EXPERIENCE
AND
ART

Teaching Children to Paint

DATE DUE			

EXPERIENCE
AND
ART

Teaching Children to Paint

NANCY R. SMITH
University of Oregon

Teachers College, Columbia University
New York and London   1983

To
Elizabeth C. Gilkeson
with affection and gratitude

Published by Teachers College Press, 1234 Amsterdam Avenue, New York, N.Y. 10027

Library of Congress Cataloging in Publication Data

Smith, Nancy R.
  Experience and art.

  Bibliography: p.
  Includes index.
  1. Painting—Study and teaching (Elementary)
2. Children as artists. 3. Children's art. I. Title.
N350.S67 1983   372.5'2   82-10287

ISBN 0-8077-2700-8

Manufactured in the United States of America

88   4   5   6

Contents

Part III.   First Representations

Part IV.   Picturing Experience

Part V.   Conclusion

Color plates appear between pages 48–49.

Foreword

Experience and Art is a lean, wise, useful book. Unlike so many books on children's drawings and paintings that emphasize on the one hand vague generalities concerning children's developmental drawing stages and on the other highly specific recipes to be followed by the would-be teacher, Nancy Smith brought theory to practice in creating a volume that speaks to those who teach children. For years in the field of art education there has been a dominant belief that children should largely be left to their own devices in art. Intervention by a well-intentioned adult was believed to be likely to stifle rather than foster the child's artistic development. In the 1960s, students of art education began to question that approach and moved gradually to one that emphasized the need to provide children with guidance and instruction and to widen the curriculum in art to which children had access. On the whole this movement away from a type of laissez-faire approach to art education was salutary. Children surely differ cognitively, socially, and emotionally from adults. This point is obvious. But one should not conclude that because of their differences their guidance by informed adults is unnecessary or, even worse, necessarily deleterious. Once having plotted some of the developmental features of children's drawings at various age levels, the task for the teacher remains. What does one do in the classroom with a three-, five-, or nine-year-old? How does one intervene? What does one say to a four-year-old, or for that matter to a fourteen-year-old about his or her paintings? Questions such as these are seldom answered in the literature. As a result, elementary school teachers, parents, and others interested in fostering the child's artistic development are largely left to their own devices. They may be offered highly prescriptive routines or descriptions of "interesting" projects. But connections between concepts, generalizations, and theories and their relationships to what one might do or say are seldom addressed. What Nancy Smith has done—and it is no small accomplishment—is to write a book filled with examples not only of what is typically produced by children of various ages, but which also contains dialogue between teachers and students, thus providing to the teacher not a recipe to follow but an example to emulate. Furthermore, these examples—portrayals of teaching episodes—are related in the gentlest way to developmental, perceptual, and cognitive theory. Calling the child's attention to an experience that he or she had during the spring is useful because meaning is important for motivation. Expression without meaning or motivation is likely to be empty, as many teachers can attest. Nancy Smith points out why questions of one sort are likely to elicit a greater and deeper response from the child than questions of another kind. She illustrates how general topics unconnected to the child's life are likely to fall flat in the classroom. Thus, she provides not a recipe but examples and theoretical principles that an intelligent lay person or teacher can employ in his or her own teaching.

Also useful in this small book are the descriptions of the kind of cues a teacher can give to a young child about his or her own painting. Rather than waxing eloquent over the array of colors or forms a child has created, the teacher uses the images that the child makes as the subject of questions, cues, and other devices designed to help the child see the relationships that are actually there. In many cases the child may not fully appreciate what he or she has in fact accomplished. Thus, the child's work becomes a source for his or her own growth while the child is in the process of producing it and it becomes a source of growth as the child is encouraged to examine it more closely. The child eventually becomes his or her own critic by learning to see what has in fact been made.

Throughout this book lies a pervasive assumption that the character of the images children make is directly related to the quality of thinking they are able to employ. Far from a deterministic view, one that accounts for performance through some unalterable mystic ability called "talent," Nancy Smith recognizes the possibilities of education, even for those under five years of age. This is as it should be. We are learning that even the prenatal environment affects the growth and development of infants. Why should it seem strange that the pedagogical environment would have little or no effect on what children are able to do or upon the kind of thinking in which they can engage? And if the forms of thinking they are able to employ do affect what they make, then why should it be surprising that teachers who have a professional responsibility to foster the development should not be important agents of change? Nancy Smith does not find such expectations surprising. Indeed, quite the contrary. Without being either a rank behaviorist or a vague romantic, she puts the problem of helping children learn to paint into a context that is at once useful and theoretically grounded. She does it without becoming tied down to prescription or lost in the ethereal quality of a cloud-filled heaven. For that achievement teachers throughout the land will be grateful. I have every reason to expect that this book will not only be appreciated by those who teach, but will also be one that will help improve the quality of art education in the classroom.

Elliot W. Eisner
Professor of Education and Art
Stanford University

Acknowledgments

From the outset I would like to acknowledge the important role Lois Lord has played in the creation of this book. She is an art educator of rare wisdom, gifted with insightful understanding of children and unfailing in her generosity to colleagues. Many years ago Lois hired me, an inexperienced young teacher, to work in the remarkable art program she had developed at The New Lincoln School in New York City. Lois took my education as a teacher in hand and revealed to me through the program itself, her teaching, and her counsel an extraordinary vision of art education. After I left New Lincoln, we continued to communicate, and later we worked together again in the Follow-Through Program at Bank Street College of Education at which time this book was first conceived. Lois has contributed those years of collaboration, hours of effort, advice, many paintings from her classes, and her fine photographs of children to this book. The spirit of her thinking is on every page.

Among the other individuals who have been instrumental in shaping my thinking and giving generously of their interest are two exceptional art educators, Jane Cooper Bland and Angiola Churchill, and two exceptional psychologists, Rudolf Arnheim and Sheldon H. White. As the years pass, my admiration for their sensitive and careful thought increases, and my gratitude for their support continues.

In addition, while working at The New Lincoln School, Bank Street College of Education, and The Art Center of The Museum of Modern Art, all in New York City, I had unusual opportunities to work toward a conception of teaching painting to children. The programs in these institutions, influenced by in-depth understanding of the theories of John Dewey and Sigmund Freud, combined some of the highest values in art and education with very perceptive observations of children's development. Sensitive scheduling, budgets for quality materials, coherent philosophy, enthusiastic and stimulating colleagues, and strong administrative support at all three made a yeasty working and learning context. I am thankful to have taught in each of them.

Over the years in these classrooms, an unusually rich body of children's art work was produced. My conviction grew that painting, properly taught, could provide children with a powerful tool for learning about the world and for creating meaning. However, it was clear that in order for this to occur, it was important that teachers be committed to this goal and know the strategies for bringing it about.

As times have changed and the world of education has grown more complex, opportunities to offer children continuity in painting activities have diminished. Art teachers have more classes with larger numbers of children in them and at the same time are asked to teach "the basics" through art, integrate the arts, and otherwise break up the little time children have for painting per se. As a consequence, teaching painting to children so as to enable them to create meaning confidently is harder to achieve. Nevertheless, those students and colleagues for whom this conviction has been nourishing have gone on to demonstrate that it can be effective in contemporary schools and with contemporary children. I want to thank all the fine students who have helped me think through this powerful form of education and all the dedicated and creative teachers who have helped to adapt it to the changing classrooms of today. In particular I want to thank the teachers in the Bank Street Follow-Through Program and in the Bank Street School for Children.

Also, I want to thank those who helped prepare the manuscript. Dennie Wolf gave many patient and thoughtful hours of editorial help, creating coherence and order when disorder threatened. Peggy Clark made the knowledgeable and charming drawings of painting setups, using her wisdom as an art teacher as well as her skill as an artist. Alex Griswold, a photographer who also understands painting, made sparkling black and white prints of the children's paintings. Celia Shneider typed the manuscript with the conscientious care of a true craftswoman. It is wonderful to have such friends.

Finally, this book continues the work of all the dedicated teachers who believe in and practice teaching painting as the creation of meaning. I hope it will prove helpful to parents, early childhood and preschool teachers, elementary classroom teachers, and, of course, to art teachers as well as to students in teacher training classes. All are invited to share the rewards of using this approach to painting as they help children to grow.

Introduction

This book has several distinctive features. First, it is based on the belief that the goal of art education is to help children achieve a better understanding of themselves and their world by using visual materials. Second, it presents an in-depth analysis of cognitive development in children's painting. Third, it offers specific techniques for teaching, consistent with its purpose, and finally, it sets out an approach to evaluation that relates children's developing abilities to creativity and basic aesthetic principles. This introduction provides an overview of the main themes and organization of the book. Each topic introduced here will be developed at greater length in following chapters.

THE CREATION OF MEANING: GOAL OF ART EDUCATION

Human beings have a basic need to organize and substantiate their thoughts and feelings. They want to make sense of their experiences and order their ideas. They do this in a number of practical, scientific, and artistic ways. The arts are different from other means of doing this, because in them it is important to consider the expressive qualities of form. The psychological function of the arts is to capture and formulate the quality, not just the objective nature, of experience. Art has become separated from the mainstream of life for most adults, but it is not so for children. Artistic expression arises naturally in children's development and is an effective mode of thought and communication for them. Thus, the primary goal of art education is to help children develop their ability to create and respond to meaning in visual imagery.

COGNITION AND PAINTING

In the past much attention has been paid to understanding the emotions that underlie children's art work. However, this book emphasizes the thinking or cognitive processes behind children's painting. The analysis of these processes is based primarily on the theories of two psychologists, Jean Piaget (e.g., 1962)* and Heinz Werner (1948). More specifically, it is based on the author's

---

*All works cited in the text are listed in the bibliography.

dissertation (Smith 1972), and differs from other accounts, notably those of Victor Lowenfeld (1947), Rhoda Kellogg (1969), and Joseph DiLeo (1970) in the depth of its examination of the role of cognition in painting.

In this analysis each phase of imagery is seen as emerging from and building on the thought processes of the previous phase. Over time, two- and three-year-olds differentiate the circle as a distinct shape from the weblike traces left by their rhythmic, circular arm movements. As a shape, the circle has unity and the spatial properties of "insideness" and "outsideness." Children embellish its border in many ways to emphasize its distinctness and spatial demarcation. A favorite embellishment is the addition of straight lines perpendicular to the border. The straight line is an early discovery, and perpendiculars are the first and favorite angle of young children. Thus, the "sun" configuration finally achieved by the four-year-old can be understood as a coordination of concepts about lines, shapes, and angles that also happens to be very striking. This kind of an approach will help teachers understand how children think about painting at different ages.

TEACHING STRATEGIES

In order for lessons to be directed toward the creation of meaning, they must be focused on the significant experiences of children. Often children need help in identifying such experiences and in thinking of them in visual terms. A specific technique of dialogue for getting children started is presented together with a specific technique for responding to children that helps them to realize more fully the meaning of their work.

EVALUATION AND AESTHETICS

Order in art, the happy balance between unity and variety, has been one of the most abiding aesthetic principles. Each period in history may have had distinctive criteria for order, but none has ignored the principle itself. This book discusses the characteristics of each phase of children's developing imagery in relation to this principle. In addition a clear distinction is drawn between the creativity of adult artists and that of children. The effort of children to find means of organizing and making images is the creativity of the child. Responsible evaluation can take place when children's order making and creativity are considered in a developmental framework.

ORGANIZATION OF THE BOOK

Part I is devoted to a general discussion of the issues introduced thus far. The application of these issues to children's development in painting is set out in Parts II, III, and IV in chapters devoted to each successive phase of growth.

Within these chapters there is the same structural sequence. Each chapter begins with a section on development titled "New Understandings About Painting"; this is followed by sections titled "Getting Started" and "Being Responsive" in which the teaching strategies are applied developmentally; the last section, "Order Making and Evaluation," discusses the aesthetic qualities of each phase and suggests procedures for evaluation. Thus, what is discussed generally in Chapter 1 is discussed specifically for each phase of development in Chapters 2 through 8.

Finally, Part V is a conclusion in which the strategies and their value for teaching the creation of meaning are discussed.

Part I
OVERVIEW

1 Painting in the Lives of Children

PAINTING AND THE CREATION OF MEANING

Children like working with materials. They are interested in finding out what each material will do and in becoming skillful in its use. At the same time children also want to make finished objects and to create images of their experiences. These interests are natural in children and adults alike; they are expressions of our human need to communicate through visual means, to feel competent, and to make sense of the world around us. These interests motivate human beings to make and respond to visual imagery, and since children have as yet little knowledge of professional art, they are able to act upon their interests directly and without inhibition. It follows, then, that the fundamental educational aim of art activities is to help children increase their capacity to create meaning and to make sense of themselves and the world around them. To achieve this end children's art activities can and should be planned so that they engage these natural interests, enhance the children's sense of competence, and enable them to reflect upon their experiences.

Art programs sometimes do not make the most of the many possible opportunities for developing competence and helping to formulate meaning. This is the case when they go no further than the surface exploration of materials and processes and when they are not focused on the life and interests of the children. Exploration needs structure and sequential lesson planning to lead to deep understanding. When such structures are omitted, fundamental learning about art and imagery is lost, and art activities become superficial "busywork." Curricula should be sequenced in such a way that children are first helped to explore the qualities of materials in depth and then helped to use this knowledge in making images of importance to them. Unless image making is directed toward concrete and personally significant experiences, there is a weak focus for the creation of meaning. In addition teachers must help to extend the range of children's experiences as a basis for painting. For art work to lead to full personal understanding and satisfaction,

3

the teacher must have a clear sense of these goals and plan experiences that move toward them.

It is the purpose of this book to offer teachers the information they need to understand and put into practice the creation of meaning as a goal for children's painting. In addition teachers will find the goal, strategies, and philosophy of evaluation applicable to their work with other materials and beyond that to other areas of the curriculum.

CHILDREN AND MATERIALS

The exuberant vitality and freshness of children's paintings excite us. We sense the expressive urges behind them, the joy children feel in exploration and accomplishment. But part of the fundamental drama of children's work in art often goes unnoticed. This is the drama of their growing understanding of visual materials.

The influence of social interactions on a developing child is often noted. We see that it is in human interactions that the child discovers and builds the satisfactions and meanings that attach to being a human being in a society of other human beings; of being a child born of mother and father; of having brothers and sisters and friends. It is in human interactions that so many wishes, needs, and ideas are developed, gratified, denied, and shared.

Interactions with materials have received less attention. However, it is in exploring materials that the child discovers the sensations, satisfactions, and meanings that attach to being human in a physical world: sensuality; cause and effect; transformations of form; the communicative properties of materials; and the pleasures and frustrations in trying to master them. The child discovers, savors, and forms ideas about the plasticity of mud, the brittle durability of rock, the intangible brilliance of light. And, as it is with social interactions, so too is it with using materials. The excitement and challenge in the interactions sustain, teach, and enrich the self. Both emotional and intellectual development are built on the evolution of these exchanges that occur with ever increasing complexity.

Through experiences with materials children build basic concepts of how the world of objects works and also of their own capacity to be effective in it. Early sensory experiences lead to later conceptual understandings of the physical world and of basic physical processes. The evolving discovery of materials takes place whether children are experimenting with pots and pans in the kitchen, a stick from the ground — or art materials. The world is abundant with materials, and as the children encounter first one and then another, they learn not only the particular nature of each but also general fundamentals about the physical world.

Infants pat their hands against the textures of blanket, water, oatmeal—mother's nose. Toddlers pile or drag everything that can be piled or dragged: cooking utensils, rocks, books, dolls, and blankets. Nursery school children select and arrange blocks, scraps, chairs, buttons, and lines of paint on paper.

Patting and touching evolves to piling and dragging which in its turn evolves to sorting and arranging.

Many of the materials children encounter lend themselves to forming images or representations, and children are quick to recognize these possibilities and adept at making use of them. For them the space under the dining room table becomes a house; a stick, an airplane. They use some materials in their original form, combine or arrange some, and manipulate others into altogether new forms. The space under the table is there, but becomes more houselike with the addition of a blanket along the edge. The stick needs only to be "flown." Chairs arranged in a line become a bus, while clay patted flat becomes a pancake.

Poster paint is chosen as a material for young children because it has flexibility, directness, and bright distinct colors. Because of these characteristics, it is easier for children to manipulate, and they can discover fundamental concepts of art more easily with it. For example, the effect of one color on another in mixing is sharply visible, or the direct relation between body movement and line is boldly presented as the child's arm bangs on a splotch of paint or wiggles through a zigzag. Poster paint also lends itself easily to the discovery of such compositional principles as repetition and variation and eventually to discovery of the representational correspondence between a drawn shape and a real object. It is also capable of considerable subtlety of tone, texture, and linear variation when used by older children; in fact, it is a fine medium for high school students. Thus, it is appropriately direct for young children while allowing them to build a foundation for more subtle work in later years. It is a medium that makes it possible to carry out strong work over a long period of the child's school life, thus helping the child to achieve greater depth and expression in the creation of meaning.

DEVELOPMENT IN PAINTING

The overview of development in painting in this section presents a schematic outline of the process, showing how each phase of learning sets the stage for the learning to follow. The discussions of development to follow in Parts II, III, and IV are more detailed and more related to practice.

The principle that each learning emerges from prior learnings is evident from the outset. In order for children to begin their development in painting at all, they must have developed a concept of tools and tool use sufficient to allow them to use brushes in a specific and specialized way. When they first begin to paint sometime during the second or third year, this capacity must be well enough established for them to dip a brush into paint and to aim their movements with it at paper. Thereafter, each step of development in painting evolves primarily as a consequence of the child's interaction with the paint itself. From very simple early manipulations children learn their first visual-graphic concepts and using them begin to work more deliberately and with greater range and flexibility. The response of the paint to these more complex manipulations reveals new, ever more subtle possibilities, and thus the process of learning takes place as a kind of dialogue between the nature of the paint and the ever growing mind of the child.

As their painting evolves, children use three distinctly different modes of thought. After the first, in which the characteristics of the visual-graphic elements—line, shape, color, and paper space—are learned, there is a second period in which children encounter the possibility of graphic representation using emotional and expressive modes of thought. In the third phase children become adept at representation using logical means of organization to create increasingly more complex images of their experiences in the world. Thus, children's concepts about paint, design, and representation build on one another. Within each of these phases there are also significant changes between earlier and later modes of thought of which to be aware. The major phases and significant changes within them are outlined in the following sections.

Learning the Elements

Motions and the Marks They Make—Ages 1½, 2, 3.   Children begin painting in basically the same way whether they are as young as one-and-a-half or as old as three. When they begin, their thoughts are focused primarily on motoric and kinesthetic sensations. The arm and body dance around and above the paper in repetitious and reflexlike movements. But the traces left by these gestures—dots, dashes, zigzags, and circular webs—are striking to the eye and begin the child's education in graphic language. The movement, continuity, and direction of line; the surface-covering property of shapes; the capacity of paints to change color when mixed; and the space of a piece of paper as a location for action all present themselves to the child who begins to take in and make use of them.

Finding Out About Lines, Shapes, and Colors — Ages 3, 4, 5.   As their visual-motor coordination increases and as their graphic concepts become more differentiated, children begin to make paintings that reveal their understanding of the capacity of lines to have particular lengths, to be oriented on paper, and to change direction moving across the paper. They begin to place colored patches in separated locations and to experiment with a variety of circular shapes. They now deliberately choose either to keep their colors clean or to mix them. They make paintings, experimenting with the repetition and variation of lines, shapes, spatial location, and color. In short, the children are gaining sufficient understanding of the basic visual-graphic elements to produce specific and varied results.

Designing — Ages 4, 5, 6.   Once children have had sufficient experience with paint to develop concepts of the basic elements, including a concept of the paper space as a continuous surface with top, bottom, center, sides, and edges, they can begin to make the elaborate combinations of lines, shapes, and colors that create the striking patterns and designs characteristic of this age level. They have the ability to cover a whole piece of paper with lines and shapes of distinct colors arranged to form an interesting well-organized whole.

Thus, the motoric activities of the first phase make possible the conceptualization of visual-graphic elements in the second phase, which makes possible the coordination of elements in the designs of phase three.

First Representations

Names for Configurations and Symbols from Designs — Ages 2, 3, 4, 5.
This phase marks the transition into representation. It begins for many children while they are making marks and continues sporadically through their acquisition of the conception of visual-graphic elements. During the second or third year, children begin to recognize similarities between the movement, emotional quality, and spatial relations of configurations they have already drawn and objects and events in the real world. However, these are fleeting moments of awareness and are not a substantial part of children's effort. An object is found in the configuration and then "named" (Lowenfeld 1947); as a consequence, there is a heterogeneous and strange variety of themes: roads, ropes, an eagle, windows, a submarine, babies, snails, a raincoat, "an alligator with a bone inside," "an elephant with a sneeze," or "Tarzan building his house."

In the next step the children modify their designs-in-progress to fit the "found" object, and then finally they select a theme before drawing. The latter they do most frequently with symbols based on designs they have made a number of times in the past. For example, typical drawings of people at this time are a circle or perhaps two circles with interior circles for facial features and lines radiating outward for arms and legs. This is a variation of the favorite design in which a circle is decorated by circles within and lines along its edge. Though produced intentionally, with the subject in mind, the form of the symbol derives more from the design rather than from thoughts of the subject.

Thus, the capacity for representation depends on the construction of concepts of visual-graphic elements and designs.

Picturing Experience

Now children choose deliberately either to create a design or to represent experience. They will continue to paint designs throughout their school years, but the thrust of their graphic activity from this time on will be in images depicting objects and events. They consciously select subjects for paintings from memories of experience using their newly developed conception of representation and conforming to their new definition of what constitutes a proper painting.

By five or six, children understand paintings, other than nonobjective paintings, to be descriptions of their interests and activities. Their narrative urge is strong, and the need to "tell the story" in painting is a powerful motivating factor to them. Then, as children's understanding of the world becomes more complex, they feel the need to represent these subtleties. They are obliged to make paintings incorporating ever more information and to devise new means for representing it. Thus, the descriptive impulse is the driving force behind the growth of their capacity for representation and expression. Whereas the need to master the medium dominated the first period of growth and the discovery of representation was the focus of the second, it is the need to describe and record events that dominates the third. Within this last period there are the three different phases sketched in the following sections.

Simple Images: People, Houses, Animals — Ages 5, 6, 7.   With the advent of more logical thought during the fifth and sixth years, the range of subjects children paint becomes organized and sharply narrowed from the earlier array of seemingly random topics. Modifying their earlier designs, children arrive at symbols using simple geometric shapes that become their characteristic way of representing basic types of objects. Since these are painted without details of sex, age, or type, it appears that children are depicting their conception of the largest category to which the object belongs. For example, images of people are "persons" of no sex, age, or profession. Later in this phase, having established symbols for basic types of objects, children move on to depicting "subcategories" (e.g., boys and girls) by adding more attributes to their basic symbols. For example, the symbol for a person becomes female with the addition of lines for a skirt and long hair.

Children combine these symbols into scenes. Typical pictures include a figure or figures on a base line with selected objects added to indicate whether the scene is outdoors (tree, sun, sky) or indoors (chair, window, table). Children's paintings at this time are also characterized by the personal quality of the events depicted; the subjects are the painter, the painter's family, and everyday experiences such as "playing in the park."

The capacity to make these images depends on the children's discovery of visual-graphic elements and the capability the elements have to represent objects and events in the real world. These discoveries taken together with the child's growing capacity for logical thought now make possible orderly and systematic representation of everyday life.

Richer Symbols: Friends, Workers, City Streets — Ages 7, 8, 9.   The variety of subjects increases as children's emerging social interests prompt them to dwell on friendships, organized sports, work, and adult responsibilities. More distant places are depicted as the children range further from home and also because their ability to internalize events experienced indirectly in books, movies, and television grows. Stories about Eskimos in far away lands and television reporting of Olympic sports come to life for them and become the themes of paintings. Individual objects as well as types or categories are depicted. The children are more mature and can conceptualize more complex entities. The themes of paintings are more subtle, the narrative more elaborate, and details richer.

Motivated by the urge to capture more information and indifferent to the laws of perspective, children combine viewpoints freely, inventing means to represent anything they wish. This freedom makes it possible for them to treat the whole paper as an organized unit of space without resolving the inherent conflict between the flatness of the paper and the roundness of experience.

Metaphors and Styles: The Den of a Wolf, A Cat on a Cushion — Ages 9, 10, 11. During this preadolescent phase, children begin to use visual images as symbols or metaphors for emotions or concepts. For example, a painting of a cat on a cushion represents the security and warmth of domesticity, while that of a mother wolf and cubs presents a picture of conflicting nurturance and aggression. Children are just becoming conscious of the capacity pictures have to refer to nonconcrete entities.

The concept of pictures with specific stylistic limitations is also developing. Children begin spontaneously to limit themselves to specific ranges of color or qualities of shape, such as simple rounded shapes for the domestic scene of a cat on a cushion. Technical skills such as using lines to create textures and shading colors to indicate shadows on a form become intrinsically interesting to them. Their curiosity about commonly accepted graphic conventions, such as those in cartoons and illustrations, intensifies; these kinds of images have styles easy to identify and tell stories that are clear and emotionally satisfying to children of this age.

Children begin to use diagonal lines to depict the edges of receding forms. They learn to use these lines from the observation of adult images without understanding the principles involved; thus, the lines lack credibility, but nevertheless indicate children's growing awareness of the convention of perspective. Their recognition of the influence of a viewpoint on an image, as indicated by their interest in painting unusual views such as those through a keyhole, binoculars, or a particular window will lead to a more substantive understanding of perspective.

In the later years of adolescence children will become even more interested in the art of their culture and want to learn many more of its techniques. This earlier phase marks the culmination of their ability to create meaning using the basic graphic language of childhood and their transition into focusing on the graphic forms of their culture.

The whole process of this evolution—the development of the ability to symbolize complex life experiences—takes from the age of two until the age of ten or eleven if children are given ample opportunity to work with paint.

The same patterns of development may occur over a shorter time span if older children are beginning to work with paint for the first time. Similarly, this sequence of development may be rehearsed again when children have had a long vacation from painting, have missed out on some necessary practice with the material, or are feeling upset. All children, whether very young, inexperienced, beginning after an absence, or suffering emotional disorientation, need to spend time exploring the basic qualities of any material. Older children may spend a few minutes mixing colors as the very young children do before the "feel" of the material is enough in their hands and minds to allow them to move on to creating images with it. Children who are upset may need to make several exploratory pictures before getting into their usual imagery.

When children have missed out on enough early painting experiences, they signal this to the teacher in several ways. They may be afraid to be free with paint; they may lack control of the paint, or they may prefer to use their painting time to swirl the brush in the water or to mix a tray full of color without ever applying it to paper. When this occurs, teachers should help children to focus on early developmental goals, for example, color mixing. They may then wish to provide all the children who demonstrate such needs with a number of opportunities to work through the learnings of earlier phases.

Teachers need to help children move along through these phases when they are ready. Often, it is hard to determine when to begin to do so. One good cue is when the children become bored and seem to lack interest or purpose in the activity they have chosen or when they are stuck in thoughtless repetition. Then the teacher can suggest a change by offering a lesson related to the next phase. If the children are ready, they will respond to it; if not, they will ignore it. The teacher should never attempt to "hurry" the children through the course of this evolution, since a superficial experience of each phase is a weak foundation for further growth. Once the proper foundation is laid, children will move on through the phases to do developmentally appropriate work easily.

THE AESTHETICS OF CHILDREN'S ART

Paintings differ from more scientific modes of communication in that part of their meaning is carried by expressive qualities of the visual-graphic elements used in composing them. The way a tree is painted—the lines, shapes, and colors the artist has selected—conveys meaning in addition to indicating the presence of a tree in the scene. The visual-graphic elements often communicate movements and/or emotional qualities such as upwardness or energy, stasis or peacefulness, weight or stability. In addition to conveying meaning simply as individual graphic elements, the way these elements are combined into a composition also communicates meaning.

In fact, artists' images present three different types of meaning woven together in an overall organization. There is a narrative strand: What is the idea or "story" being presented? This strand is present whether the painting is objective or nonobjective, since nonobjective paintings by adults represent concepts purely through lines, shapes, and colors (as for example, a presentation of serenity in geometric forms contrasted with tensions created by their irregular arrangement, in many of Mondrian's paintings). There is an emotional strand: What are the feelings communicated by the narrative and by the visual-graphic elements? And, there is a compositional strand: What sort of visual interest and unity are created by the arrangement of graphic elements, the lines, shapes, and colors? The overall organization should weave each of these strands into a unified whole and convey a clear meaning.

The aesthetic value of a painting is usually determined by assessing the quality of the meaning and organization in each of these strands and the whole. For example, as part of the narrative of several of his great paintings of Mont Sainte-Victoire, Cezanne depicted the rugged mountain beyond a fertile and tranquil landscape, and he painted portions of a tree in the near space, thus locating the viewer firmly at a point in the foreground and at some distance from the mountain. He gave emotional flavor to these scenes by using interrupted lines, block shapes, and fresh, vibrant colors that add power to the forms in the landscape and excitement to the brilliant light. In the design of the compositions, he created tension between opposing characteristics, as powerful movements into space are contrasted with stabilizing vertical and horizontal movements. The overall effect of these contrasts in narrative, emotional, and compositional qualities is to confront the viewer with a charged and transcendent image of the tension between the power and the serenity of nature (and art).

Is it appropriate—or helpful—to look at children's art in this way? At first glance it seems that orchestration of these strands into a satisfying whole is too complex a task for children. The study of development in children's painting shows that their paintings are based on but a few ideas and that their ability to organize them grows slowly. But it also shows that their images do convey emotions and do strive for unity. In fact, their capacity to integrate the narrative, emotional, and compositional aspects of a painting surpasses that of most adults since these strands have not yet become separated for them.

The emotional qualities communicated by visual-graphic elements are self-evident to young children, who are innately attuned to the expressive qualities in these elements. They perceive that lines jump excitedly across the paper or that a color shouts out noisily. In addition when children first begin to discover representation, it is these expressive qualities, together with a few very simple spatial properties, that they use as the basis of depiction. The massive bulk of an elephant is created by a group of bulging arcs rather than by a contoured outline. In this mode of depiction bulginess is equated with bulginess—and there is no separation of graphic means and content. Finally, children begin very early to feel the need for composition, selecting and arranging graphic elements to create simple types of order and interest, first in nonrepresentational and then in representational paintings. Thus, despite the simplicity of their narrative and organizational means, children can and do create meaning and aesthetic order in their paintings, and it is helpful to examine their work within this framework.

At the same time children exercise these aesthetic understandings within developmental limits, and adults must learn to recognize the types of meaning and organization appropriate to each phase in the sequence of development. In order to be able to do this, it is important to study the course of children's art closely (as we will do in the sections to follow) and to follow the creative process of each child within individual paintings and over sequences of paintings. The children's intentions, their focus of interest, and the range of conceptual and technical means at their disposal can be identified. Then the question may be asked: Within the limits of their ability and intention, what kinds of relationships have they used to create variety and unity? Based on this evaluation, the teacher can be responsive to children's aesthetic abilities.

As the children develop more capacity for organized thought and as they are more influenced by adult conceptions, form and content become more differentiated for them. During the years from six to eight, they seem primarily concerned with content, focusing their conscious efforts on "telling the story," and generally do not consciously use expressive properties to indicate emotional qualities, even though the topics they choose are very meaningful to them. A visit to the dentist may be painted as brightly as a visit to grandmother. However, even during this time they can respond with understanding and interest to questions and suggestions about the expression and organization of a painting. Later, once the separation of the two strands is well established, between eight and ten, they begin to make deliberate relations between form and content using the expressive properties of visual-graphic elements consciously and with more variety and subtlety. For example, they consciously employ darker tones of a color to suggest an unhappy mood or deliberately use very smooth and graceful lines to convey elegance.

In western thought we have come to make a sharp separation between the cognitive and affective. But, no matter how objective adults try to be, both the cognitive and affective are intertwined in our thought. Painting and the other arts acknowledge and celebrate this interdependence, rather than ignore it. In paintings by adults there is a balance of knowing and feeling, a recognition of the necessity of each, and a formulation of the relationship between them through the organization of the relation of form and content. The powerful character of lines and shapes in the Cezanne landscape conveys the artist's feelings about the landscape as well as his convictions about the importance of structure in the composition of paintings. The origin of this relationship can be found in young children's fusion of thought and feeling and in their perception of expressive properties in both objects and graphic configurations.

The differentiation of thought and feeling in imagery occurs in the same pattern of fusion, separation, and reintegration we observed for form and content. For the four- or five-year-old, subject and mood are one. By six or seven, emotions related to essentials of the narrative may be depicted literally; the reaching arm is longer, the important person is bigger, and the new dress more decorated. These are expressive emphases in imagery and differ from emotional qualities conveyed by expressive use of line, shape, and color per se. In preadolescence the child begins to picture emotions as themes in and of themselves. Images of a solitary figure are titled "Loneliness," or of two figures "Friendship." Finally, thought and feeling, having been separated, can be purposefully joined through the relation of expressive qualities in the material to the theme.

Parenthetically, it is important to note that the expression of emotions with little or no attempt at organization does not constitute working in an aesthetic, artistic process. It does not produce relationships between thought and feeling or between form and content. It also does not, if continued over time, contribute to the health of the child since the resolution of conflict and confusion is not found through such work.

Behind the third sort of organization, composition of visual-graphic elements, is the innate human desire for order. All methods of creating order do so by forming systematic relationships between the objects or facts to be organized. Any artist selects and arranges lines, shapes, and colors to create a sense of order and unity. Children make order chiefly by using repetition and variation of graphic elements. Their ability to organize elements develops naturally. Three-year-olds repeat the same kind of lines and shapes on top of each other on the paper, creating an inadvertent order. Later, they scatter similar lines or shapes over the paper. Still later, children can place varied elements in similar locations on the paper. Finally, the beautifully organized designs typical of four- and five-year-olds are based on these similarities and differences of line, shape, color, and location. Later, in representational paintings, children organize these elements both to depict objects and events and to achieve interesting and unified compositions.

A final note of caution. Because children's work appears fresh and spontaneous, it has often been misinterpreted by writers and artists. This look of freshness is understood as if children had the same skills, motivations, and knowledge of art as adults. But adult artists' social and cultural ideas about art do not exist for the young child. Children have no preconceived ideas about art from which to achieve freedom; rather, children lack such ideas. Their effort is to gain control over fragments of sensations, feelings, and ideas; thus, what appears to an adult as direct and spontaneous is apt to be the consequence of developing mastery of the medium on the part of the child.

Children's work *is* related to artists' work in a more straightforward and yet profound way. In it the fundamentals of art are revealed in pure and simple form. In it we can trace the basic characteristics of art back to their psychological origins. For example, movement is an inherent property of line; speed and direction are of its essence. In the art work of children, line begins as the almost accidentally leftover trace of a movement. Similarly, rhythm is an equally inherent property of graphic repetitions. It appears in the first gesture-marks that children make. These graphic characteristics, movement and rhythm, are basic in human perception, and children begin to understand and make use of them in art when they are very young. In these examples and many others, children's work reveals the bedrock foundations of art, those foundations that have their sources in the physical nature of materials, in perception and human emotion, and that exist irrespective of the whims of history.

Just as we must not view children's work as the result of a remarkable artistic spontaneity unique to children, so also must we not view it as failed adult work. To find child art inept and confused is to misunderstand the difference between child art and fine art and to ignore the developmental process that takes place in children. Children starting with no conception of the basic visual-graphic elements, of making images, of a finished product, or of art as communication must, through trial and error, build an understanding of each of these fundamental aspects of art. Each phase of this sequence of experimentations produces its own appropriate intentions, skills, system of organization, and imagery. Our task is to come to understand the child's thought and purpose—and to view the work accordingly. In fact, we will see in the chapters that follow how understanding children's thought informs the procedures teachers use to start painting sessions, to be responsive to children, and then eventually to evaluate children's progress.

Part II
LEARNING THE ELEMENTS

2 Motions and the Marks They Make

AGES 1½, 2, 3

NEW UNDERSTANDINGS ABOUT PAINTING

Children's first experiments with paint begin with many rhythmic brushings back and forth across the paper. They continue this for so long sometimes that the paper is worn through from the vigor and repetition of strokes. They have no idea that paint colors can mix or be guided to make lines and shapes. They experience the kinesthetic sensation of their arm movement, the tactile sensation of the paint brush, and then discover marks produced on the paper. Often they gaze around the room while their arm swings to and fro. From time to time they may change the brush from one hand to the other. They have not as yet developed handedness and prefer to paint with the hand closest to the area being painted. The marks pile on top of each other and begin to form a solid mass of grey-brown, as distinct colors become mixed indiscriminately in the flurry of action. But through this motoric activity children begin to learn that paint can make lines, that its separate colors are mixable, that it can be made to form shapes. These visual-graphic phenomena inevitably appear in front of the children as they move the brush and begin to capture their interest.

Rod painted his first painting at about three years of age (Plate I). He painted on an 18″ x 24″ piece of white paper working at a table; the primary colors, black, and white were on his tray, and he had one brush, rinse water, and a sponge (see Appendix: Painting Setups). First, he dipped his brush in red and moved it back and forth touching the paper. Then he dipped his brush in all the colors, dipping from one to the next, right after each other. He put the paint-filled brush on the paper and spread the paint further and further. As he added more and more paint in repeated applications, the paper became covered with the grey mixture. Brushing even more vigorously now that there was a large pool of paint, he dug several holes in the paper. He might have continued brushing even longer, but at this point the teacher suggested he might like to have a new piece of paper.

Looking at the results of his enthusiastic activity, we can see how repeated experiences of this kind will lead him to discover the properties of paint. During the next months he will learn that paints change color if you mix them and otherwise do not. He will not learn to produce specific colors until sometime later. Rod's movements have also left traces of lines and shapes in the paint, which in time he will begin to recognize. These early smeared and puddled paintings are the children's first laboratory experiments to discover the visual-graphic properties of paint.

Experimentation with paint usually begins when children enter pre-school or kindergarten. Often they have already been drawing with crayons and pencils for some time and can produce lines and shapes in these media readily. Nevertheless, consistent with the laws of development, they must begin at the beginning in paint, with rhythmic, motoric actions. Thus, they have little or no intention of producing lines, shapes, or specific colors with paint, even though their ability to draw in crayon may be more developed. They are not lagging behind, but simply building up necessary knowledge in the paint itself.

Stimulated by their pleasure in "the feel" of paint, by their interest in the mysterious phenomenon of making colors change, and by making marks appear where none were before, the children continue to paint and experiment. Paintings are made with but a few strokes on them as children use swiping motions such as Rachel, 3:4,* did on dark paper (Figure 1); with scatterings of dots as children push the brush repeatedly against the paper (cf. Figure 2; Hess, 3:6); with a mass of mixed colors in which the tangled traces left by circular and zigzag arm motions can be seen (cf. Plate I; Rod, 3:1); and with one or more patches of color (cf. Figure 3; Jimmy, 3:5). Some children may paint for a few minutes, others for as long as half an hour. Some may use quite a few pieces of paper while others will want only one or two.

Eventually they purposefully try to produce the lines and shapes their body movements have produced earlier by accident. A circular shape may first appear because of children's usual gestures with the arm, but in a short time children can produce a series of planned variations on the theme of circles. It is in this way that children begin their systematic investigation of the visual-graphic elements.

Line, shape, and color are sensory phenomena that must be recognized and built up as concepts in order to guide actions in painting. Moving with the material and watching its responses is integral to this learning process. Children's learning is helped most if they use brushes directly as an extension of the arm. This occurs when they are given one brush and water in which to rinse it. The physical action of reaching with arm and brush to select from the array of paints helps to teach colors and concepts of color. Working with a

---

*The younger children's ages are given by year and month; thus, Rachel was three years and four months when she painted Figure 1. The older children's ages are indicated by school grade.

Figure 1.   Gesture-Marks.   Rachel, 3:4.

Figure 2.   Dots and Patches.   Hess, 3:6.

Figure 3.   A Patch and a Mark.   Jimmy, 3:5.

single brush and learning to rinse (which most of them will master in a few weeks) gives children direct control over their color choices and greater understanding of the fluidity of paint.

Since the children's attention is focused on the motoric and tactile sensations of painting, they sometimes appear to be doing messy and muddy work. But this work is essential to the sound growth of their future skills and ideas. Through early motoric work, solid foundations are established, visual-motor coordination increases, and children begin to guide the brush more and more in relation to visual-graphic concepts.

GETTING STARTED

For beginners the paint itself is enough stimulus. The teacher helps by setting out the paints invitingly, by organizing the work space conveniently so that materials are within easy reach, and by providing paint that is smooth and workable. Thick paint, the consistency of heavy cream, allows children to control the paint more easily and to explore many possibilities of thickness and thinness, by using it as it is or by adding water. Also, if the children are working at an easel, thicker paint helps to reduce the number of drips.

In the beginning the teacher can explain the simple routines of painting to the children until they become familiar with them. The teacher can show the children or help them go through dipping the brush in paint, applying it to paper and also washing it. "Before you take a new color, wash your brush in the bottom of the water jar (this reduces splashing). Next, wipe it on the edge of the jar and then dry it on the sponge (the presence of the sponge is very effective in reminding the children to wipe the brush and also absorbs the remaining water). Then dip into a new color."

It may take weeks or months before all three-year-olds remember to wash the brush each time before they dip it into a new color, but most are interested in the process almost immediately. However, too much insistence on washing the brush can inhibit the development of beginners, since young children often get immediate pleasure from the feel of paint as they dip from one container to the next. If a child is involved and derives pleasure from the process, it is not very important that the paints are becoming muddy, if the quantities are small. On the other hand, if a child continues dipping from color to color in an overly excited or noninvolved way, the teacher can help with a gentle reminder to "wash your brush and wipe it on the sponge." Sometimes it helps when the teacher brings the child a set of fresh colors, "Here are some bright new colors to use along with those you have mixed— they will stay bright if you wash your brush before you take a new color." The key to the value of the experience is the child's interest and involvement. Taking ample time to watch as a child begins to understand paint is a supportive act in itself. Observation also helps teachers to understand the process the child is going through.

Most very young children mix different colors of paint together on their papers. This results not only in dark and blended paintings, but in brushes with dark and blended colors on them. These inevitably find their way into the paints, and for this reason it is wise to put very little color in each jar of paint so that they can be cleaned easily.

Children who paint for the first time when they are six or seven may need specific suggestions and encouragement to try mixing colors and to work in an experimental way. As with the very young children, it is the process that is important. The seven-year-old may spend a first session mixing colors with no attempt to arrange or organize them. The teacher might suggest different ways of applying paint to this child on the next occasion. Older children do not stay as long in an earlier phase and may even pass through several phases in one day's lesson.

BEING RESPONSIVE

In this first stage it is particularly important that the teacher's responses refer to the processes involved and their results. "How beautiful" or "You have made a pretty picture" is not relevant. Indeed, comments such as these have no meaning for a child who has been concentrating on the physical sensations of the material. More observant responses concern the child's motor activity and the resulting visual aspects of the work. Comments might be: "You like the feel of the paint, don't you?" "How did you make your brush make dots?" "See how you changed the colors by mixing them together." "How did you move your arm to make this line?"

If the teacher watches a child working, it is easier to understand the child's thought and respond to it. As the child begins to discover what it is possible to make the paint brush do, the teacher can reinforce the child's learnings. For example: "Look, here is a patch of yellow, how bright it looks next to the grey color," or to another child, "Let's look, where did you make lines and where did you make shapes?" or "You made the dots go all around." Descriptive comments about children's work help to bring into their conscious awareness the visual consequences of their physical experiments. It also helps children to formulate their concepts and remember them if the teacher offers names for them and validates the children's thought by recognizing the thrust of their efforts.

Putting up a display of children's paintings is worthwhile even though these very young children soon forget which painting is theirs and what it felt like to paint it. Displaying their work communicates to children that the teacher values and respects their ideas and also helps to establish the classroom as the child's place of work and learning. An array of paintings also helps the children and teachers (and parents) to look at and discuss art work and to continue their discovery of the characteristics of visual-graphic elements, as they live with them and discuss them individually and in meetings.

When a painting is displayed, the child's name may be written on a card and placed on the wall directly below it. This is preferable to a teacher writing the name on the front of the painting itself. The picture surface belongs to the child and is the child's to design; a name written by someone else interferes with that design. Alternatively, teachers may write children's names on the backs of their paintings.

ORDER MAKING AND EVALUATION

At this stage when there is a minimum of visual planning and control, the dominant aesthetic aspects of the children's work are the pleasure they take in the activity and their dawning recognition of the expressive properties of marks. Since children's development in painting begins in the process of moving with the material (not in making products), it is appropriate to evaluate growth on the basis of the children's increasing confidence, sense of involvement, and competence as shown by the greater variety and control of these movements. The teacher will get a good sense of the individual child's working styles, interest, and assurance by watching the posture and expression of each child at work.

Teachers can show their pleasure and appreciation by responding to the children's pleasure. They can comment on the children's effort, interest, or delight and also on their body movements, whether they be rhythmic or irregular, quick or slow, soft or strong. They can comment on the expressivity of the graphic elements that can be seen in the paintings, the cheerfulness of bright colors and the peacefulness of neutral colors, the delicacy of little shapes and the heaviness of large shapes, the energy of jagged lines and the soothing swing of rocking lines. Communication of their pleasure and understanding helps teachers to build a shared sense of concern for painting with the children.

3 Finding Out About Lines, Shapes, and Colors

AGES 3, 4, 5

NEW UNDERSTANDINGS ABOUT PAINTING

In this phase the child explores specific qualities of lines, shapes, and colors. Are lines straight or curved? Do they wander roving over the paper or march along parallel each one to the next (cf. Figure 4; Ira, 4:2)? Are they separated or do they cross? Are there long lines and short ones?

Now, with more visual-motor control and dawning awareness of the visual-graphic elements, children begin a much more deliberate series of experiments as one discovery in the material leads to the next. They discover the capacity of paint to cover a specifically shaped area of paper surface (cf. Figure 5; Ronny, 3:10) and explore possible shapes through variations on circles. They paint big and little, touching and not touching circles; circles inside each other; filled and empty circles; circles with marks inside; and circles decorated along the edge (cf. Figure 6; John, 4:9). They make irregular or rambling shapes (cf. Figure 7; Amy, 3:6) and also squares or rectangles (cf. Figure 8; Donny, 4:8). Often they try to keep colors separate, using them directly from the container and changing from one to the next with each stroke (now brush washing gains more meaning). They may mix colors deliberately or use colors that have become mixed by accident, but keep them unmixed with further colors. Pink is a mixture that appeals to many children at this time.

In their effort to expand their knowledge and gain control of the medium, the children follow observable working procedures. They often repeat a configuration over the paper; later they may paint a single larger version of it in the middle of another paper. Or, they may paint variation after variation as their interest in a particular graphic configuration unfolds over weeks or months.

Figure 4. Parallel Lines. Ira, 4:2.

Figure 5. A Large Shape. Ronny, 3:10.

Figure 6.   John (4:9) Painting Circles.   Photo by Lois Lord.

Figure 7.   Lines, Shapes, and Colors in Separated Locations.   Amy, 3:6.

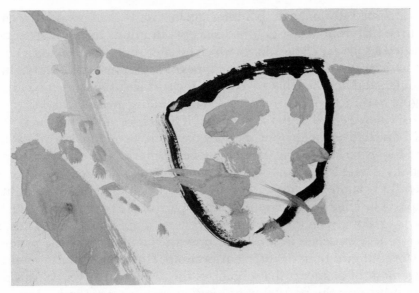

Figure 8.   A Rectangle with Shapes Inside.   Donny, 4:8.

A child may select one or two graphic concepts to contrast in a single painting (cf. Plate II; Billy, 3:6) as we can discover by following Billy's painting process.

Holding the brush in his left hand, Billy dipped it in the yellow paint. He looked at it thoughtfully and then placed the brush carefully in the upper center of the paper. He scrubbed the brush back and forth making a patch of yellow, then rinsed it and stirred it around in the red. He paused, brush suspended, and then placed it with deliberation on the lower right edge of the paper and drew it with slow care horizontally across the lower quarter of the paper. He repeated this horizontal stroking several times as he extended the line further and further across the paper. For each of these strokes he used red and made a single horizontal motion revealing his intentions quite clearly. He stopped as another child spoke to him but then refocused easily on the painting, looking it over. Now he dipped first in the yellow, then in the blue, and painted the resulting green over the yellow patch with separate repeated parallel strokes. When the yellow patch was covered, he began moving the brush in a carefully articulated path down the left side of the paper, pulling the brush first in one direction and then another so that each successive angle differed from the one before it. Occasionally the line crossed itself and enclosed shapes resulted. Once it crossed over the tip of the red line. When the line had returned to it-self, up under the large solid patch, he rinsed his brush and dipped it in red and then white. He painted several strokes of this pink over the now green patch and the pink became purple-grey as it mixed with the green. He looked thoughtfully at the painting for a moment and then put his brush down.

Watching Billy make the painting and looking at it afterward, it seems he had three different visual-graphic concepts in mind. In the first sequence he created a solid patch of color to which he later returned, making it darker. He then drew two distinctly different types of lines, one that was straight and horizontal, and another that roved over the surface of the paper continually changing its direction relative to itself. The painting presents the contrast of a patch of color created by parallel lines with two types of isolated lines.

When children begin to paint, they paint stroke on top of stroke without regard for visual and spatial separation of each mark. Now configurations are placed in different positions on the paper. In order to present his three ideas clearly, Billy painted them at the center top, lower left, and lower right, for example. The children's awareness of the space of the paper surface has been developing along with their awareness of line, shape, and color. Thus, they now confine themselves to working within the boundaries of the paper and can place configurations on different locations. However, they cannot plan an arrangement of elements that organizes the whole paper yet. In this phase children discover the possibility of locating lines, shapes, and colors in the center, at the top, to the left or right; in the next they will begin to make planned use of these locations to organize designs and compositions.

Out of the earliest motoric experimentations and the visual discoveries made possible by coordination of eye and hand, children construct basic conceptions of the visual-graphic elements and their possible positioning on the surface of the paper. In these discoveries they have used two fundamental principles as a basis of experimentation: *repetition* and *variation*. As their capacity to repeat and vary the type and location of configurations expands, these two principles will provide the key to control over the design or composition of paintings. Repetition and variation are the foundation principles of all designing, and it is these principles the child uses in the next phase to create unified designs.

GETTING STARTED

At this time, in addition to the beginning techniques, the teacher can do much to encourage the discovery of new awareness by supplying a careful selection of different materials and tools. Different sizes and shapes of paper help to stimulate the children's thinking about the space of the paper surface. Painting on colored paper (cf. Figure 1; Rachel 3:4) invites attention to the spaces between shapes and to color relationships. The teacher can offer the children a different size of brush to work with for several weeks, allowing them to discover differences in the thickness and flexibility of lines. The children can be offered different places to paint: on the floor, at a table, or on a large piece of paper on the wall. Each of these brings different portions of the body into play. Paper as large as 24″ × 36″ on the wall is very helpful when a child is becoming more aware of placing elements on the paper because it presents a surface about the size of the child for consideration. Each new experience should be offered by itself with an ample time period allowed for experimentation. It may take the children several weeks of experimentation with big and little pieces of paper to discover and assimilate the configurations each makes possible.

In offering changes of paper, brushes, or painting locations the teacher can call the children's attention to the new material and invite them to experiment with them. "Do you want a long piece or a square piece of paper? Do you want to place your long paper sideways or up and down? What kind of strokes can you make on a long paper?" The teacher should try to ask simple, fundamental questions and to offer as few suggestions as possible. The purpose of the questions is to focus the children on the characteristics of the material so that they may begin their own experimentation with them.

There is one aspect of painting in which limiting the selection of materials too narrowly may not be helpful to children. It may seem that children would gain a sense of colors and color mixing more quickly if paints were set out a few at a time. But children are often distressed by the absence of the other basic (primary) colors and become less involved in their work. This may be because their response to color is so strong and they feel the loss of one or another color very much. Or perhaps, since their learning process is based on the differentiation of characteristics, it may be that omitting primary colors makes too narrow a range for them to experiment with. In any case it has proven most supportive of children's learning to offer them the primaries and black and white. Thus, they have no extraneous colors but can discover all the basic combinations of hue and all the variations of those hues as they become lighter with white and darker with black.

By now most children have developed the skill to wash their brushes and mix colors on the tray and/or paper. They discover how to make orange, green, and purple as well as browns, greys, pinks, and other light colors. Sometimes children ask how to mix a color. In answering, it is helpful to support the child's independent discovery process. The teacher can point to several of the colors asking which of them is needed and suggesting that the child try mixing them to see if they produce the desired result. Also, children often help each other as they share in the excitement of making "new colors."

BEING RESPONSIVE

A brief conversation after a painting is finished helps bring into conscious knowledge the ideas the child has been grappling with. Framing a descriptive comment helps the teacher to look more closely and to understand the interests and intentions of the child. In their discussion teacher and child share views. The teacher gains more insight and is thus better able to validate the learning and experience of the child.

The teacher can talk to the children specifically about different characteristics of the visual-graphic elements, their repetitions and variations. For example, a teacher might say to Ira, 4:2 (Figure 4), "All your lines go up and down. How does the edge of the paper go? How did you move your arm to make the lines go up and down like the edge of the paper? Where did you start this line? Can you point to the beginning and the end of each line?"

To Billy, 3:6 (Plate II), a teacher might say, "You made a big shape on your paper. Did you use a lot of colors to make the shape? Can you remember which colors you used?"

To Donny, 4:8 (Figure 8), a teacher might comment, "You made lines, shapes and dots, didn't you? Where is the biggest shape you made? What kinds of lines did you make inside it? Is there a shape inside it? What kinds of marks did you make outside the big shape?"

It is important to supply the children with the words they will need to be able to discuss their work with the teacher. For example, children need the names of the visual-graphic elements, their particular characteristics, and the ways of organizing them. The children should be able to use such phrases as "straight, curved, and wiggling lines; light and dark colors; round, rectangular, bumpy, and smooth shapes; top, bottom, and middle of the paper." Such terms give children the vocabulary to identify what they have done and to communicate with the teacher and each other.

ORDER MAKING AND EVALUATION

Children's developing understanding of graphic possibilities makes it possible to produce configurations with a wide variety of expressive features. Some are bold, some delicate, some straightforward; others are elusive or tranquil. Teachers should look for much greater variety in lines and shapes, for clear as well as mixed and neutral colors, and for the placement of configurations in different locations on the paper space. Children's attention span and interest varies considerably at this time. Some children may lose interest in painting for several weeks at a time, some will sustain intense interest, and others will have little interest. If a whole group of children seems to lack interest, it is often because the teacher has inadvertently communicated little value for painting. One remedy is for the teacher to be sure to stay in the painting area while the children work. The children will recognize this as a sign of the importance the teacher places on the painting activity and start to give it more of their own attention.

Ordinarily, the natural pleasure and satisfaction of increasing competence motivates the children and reinforces their growing capacity to experiment in logical sequences, creating paintings in which order is derived from the child's focus on one or two ideas about visual-graphic elements. The result of such focus is the creation of very simply unified works. There may be few paintings organized into a whole design or composition, but most paintings will display the child's thoughts on several visual-graphic ideas, such as the positioning of parallel vertical lines or the contrast between lines and shapes.

Now the children's pleasure in mastery is more evident. Marks and shapes and colors are the result of knowledge and forethought. Imagine the extraordinary thrill of discovery as the child experiences for the first time the transformation of a pale puddle of white paint into a vibrant pink, simply by adding a bit of red. What an even greater sense of power to be able to make pink—or other colors—at will. One of the profoundest rewards of young children's work with paint is their developing sense of themselves as active and competent agents, able to interact and be effective in the world. In evaluating their activities and paintings teachers should look for this growing assurance, as well as for the wider range and more focused character of children's visual ideas.

4 Designing

AGES 4, 5, 6

NEW UNDERSTANDINGS ABOUT PAINTING

All paintings are a layer of paint applied in an arrangement of lines, colors, and shapes on a flat surface. In all types of painting one of the basic aesthetic problems is planning this arrangement to create an interesting but unified composition. Very young children's paintings have a kind of unity that derives from the limited range of their ideas and from their singleness of purpose at any given time. However, as their conception of line, shape, and color grows, their capacity for selecting and organizing these elements also increases. Children are developmentally tuned to deliberate exploration of new phenomena, and this innate and purposeful focusing provides their work with logic and order. They often begin with a shape or mark discovered earlier and take it as a theme for the whole picture. The theme may be a particular angle or combination of angles, a pattern of zigzags or parallel lines, a contrast of regular or irregular shapes; as this theme is repeated and revised over the paper, children also begin to make the configurations fit together as a whole on the paper. They often cover most of the paper with shapes and colors, but when they do not, they seem to place shapes on the paper carefully so that the unpainted portions contribute to the whole design. As they develop a wider range of knowledge from which to address the question of unity, children take on greater responsibility for organizing their work.

This change in children's approach to painting is clear both from their work and from their working processes. Since they now compose the design from a particular view, they reject suggestions to turn their paper around (enabling them to reach distant portions of the paper when working at a table). When asked if they are finished, children also often reject a new piece of paper until they have considered the painting carefully and decided whether it is just the way they want it or needs more work. While painting, they keep their eyes focused on the tip of the brush, moving it with delibera-tion through a series of carefully articulated gestures to build up the pattern piece by piece. While working, the children pause, brush suspended, regard-ing their work. The attentive tilt of their heads, the containment of still energy in their bodies, the alertness of their backs, and the focus of their faces —all of these physical clues reveal their interest, involvement, and concentration. The results of this concentration and deliberation are revealed in the careful order of their designs.

Libby, 4:5 (Figure 9), painted a series of rectangles of different sizes and proportions fitted together first by outlining and then filling in. She painted the radiating lines at the right by first painting a vertical and a horizontal perpendicular to it. Thereafter, she bisected the resulting 90 degree angles and then the resulting 45 degree angles. The consequence of her planful division of the angles is a very even array of lines.

The Paper as a Continuous Surface

Underlying children's interest in unified compositions is their growing conceptualization of the surface space of the paper. Originally, children approach the paper space as a vaguely distinguished arena in which to play, a sort of two-dimensional park; as they grow, children come to understand the paper as a continuous surface with discrete perpendicular edges, horizontal and vertical axes, and an infinite number of locations upon which graphic elements may be positioned. Recognition of the unity and divisability of the

Figure 9.   A Design of Rectangles.   Libby, 4:5.

paper surface brings with it recognition of the paper surface as one of the graphic elements requiring organization and offering variety. In other words, the paper's physical surface makes the problem of unity visible and concrete to the child.

Recognition of the continuity and unity of the paper surface brings with it a second realization. In order to cover a whole piece of paper with different colors, it is necessary to paint the edge of one shape up against the edge of another. Sometimes children do this by filling in shapes they have outlined (cf. Figure 10; Melissa, 4:10) and sometimes by painting one shape directly up against another (cf. Figure 11; James, 5:10). In both circumstances technical skill is required so that the wet boundaries of each color do not bleed into each other and blur. Cognitively, this requires a sophisticated concept of reciprocal boundaries between shapes, in which one edge is understood to stand as the definition of two shapes simultaneously. Children employ this concept of reciprocal boundaries in paintings in which geometric shapes are fitted together (cf. Figure 9); in paintings in which bold, clear free-form shapes are fitted together (cf. Figure 11); and in paintings rich in variety and texture. For example, in a very sensuous painting (Plate III; Alan, grade 1), a large white arc is tucked around a circular shape of blue inside a golden border. Many smaller shapes are tucked in between these larger ones, and the whole is fitted together like a jigsaw puzzle. In order to make this painting it was necessary for Alan to understand that the white and blue, as well as other, shapes would retain their distinctness and identity, even if only one line served to define their edges.

The concept of shared boundaries is difficult for children to accept as they have just learned to position shapes separately, out over the paper surface. The shapes that were at first lost in a flurry of brush strokes have become sharp and distinct because the children have learned to position them in different locations (cf. Plate II; Billy, 3:6) and they appear reluctant to lose this newly gained clarity. Often a child hesitantly brushes islands of color closer and closer to each other across a span of blank paper, until, finally, shape is meshed against shape. Nevertheless, children are drawn to making shapes that touch and yet remain distinct. Once they have conceptualized shapes as discrete entities and the paper surface as continuous and divisible, the use of shared boundaries seems to emerge naturally.

The clarity of children's eventual understanding of joining shapes on the paper space is probably most clearly revealed in paintings rich in texture (cf. Figure 12; Sally, grade 1). In this painting each of the shapes is distinct in spite of the blendings and brushings Sally used to create a variety of textures. The control needed to keep the edges from blurring is based on understanding that the viscosity of poster paint allows it to be "buttered" on. This same understanding is used in making these kinds of "wet-in-wet" textures. Thus, the deliberate use of controlled textures and shared boundaries is apt to emerge at about the same time.

Figure 10.   Melissa (4:10) Mixing Colors and Filling in a Shape.
Photo by Lois Lord.

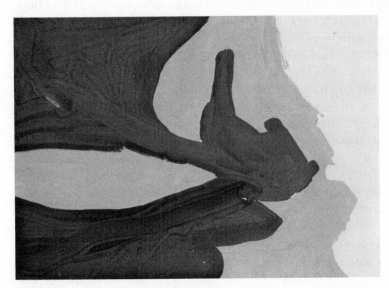

Figure 11.   Bold Shapes with Shared Boundaries.   James, 5:10.

Figure 12. Design with Texture and Numbers. Sally, grade 1.

Repetition and Variation

Another development that makes possible greater flexibility in producing unity is the ability to repeat and vary geometric shapes. The children have taught themselves to make circles of many types and to put them in many locations on the paper (cf. Figure 6; John, 4:9). Their studies of vertical and horizontal lines and the intersection of these lines have led them to make rectangles of many sizes and proportions (cf. Figure 9; Libby, 4:5). These shapes along with the triangle constitute a vocabulary of basic shapes. This vocabulary can be varied in color, size, proportion, and location, making it possible for children to create interesting as well as unified designs with very simple means.

In the future the capacity to vary geometric shapes becomes one of the underpinnings of the child's early representations. Through combination of these basic shapes in appropriate arrangements and sizes, children of five, six, and seven represent their experiences. Houses are represented by rectangles with triangles on top; girls have circles for heads and triangles for body-dresses; trees are circles with slender rectangles beneath them. While these images appear later, the facility children gain in drawing and joining shapes of different sizes and proportions at this time leads to their later representational ability.

With ever increasing ability to create variety and complexity in patterns, the child begins to make designs that remind adults of "abstract art." This is an understandable interpretation. The children have begun to use all the basic pictorial elements, even though they have not yet begun to represent. To a trained eye their use of these elements is in a young and simple form even though their deliberate and expressive use of visual-graphic elements and unified organization is suggestive of adult work.

To equate children's work with that of adults is misleading in several respects. As far as children are concerned, there is nothing abstract about their work. They have not yet become so wedded to representation that its absence seems "abstract," quite the contrary. Lines, shapes, colors, and paper space are the real stuff of painting, and organizing them is a concrete not an abstract activity. Further, adult abstract art and children's designs differ from each other in that children's art is simply a design, while adult works are metaphorical statements of thoughts and feelings the artist wished to convey in a nonliteral way. Moreover, adult paintings are influenced by history and culture. Young children's paintings do not have metaphorical meaning; they are made without knowledge of history and are simply examples of order making with visual-graphic means.

GETTING STARTED

In this phase the materials and the child's developing knowledge of organizing the picture surface provide the motivation. Since these children are particularly concerned with the arrangement of lines, colors, and shapes on the picture surface, it continues to be appropriate to offer various sizes, proportions, and colors. It is challenging for them to solve the problem of arranging rectangles on a proportion other than the usually provided 18" × 24" or 18" × 12" paper. They can try square or long and narrow paper; paper placed either horizontally or vertically; and so forth. The teacher can ask a simple question about arrangement such as, "You have chosen a long narrow piece of paper—I wonder how you will arrange shapes on it?" The interest and support of the teacher continues to be important. Similarly, the teacher's knowlege of each child's current interests makes it possible to encourage the child to continue in his or her own way. A simple question or two from the teacher may help. Following are some examples.

> "Yesterday you mixed new colors for your picture. Do you want to use some of those colors or make some new ones today? How will you start?"
>
> "There are many kinds of lines — curvy lines, straight lines, wandering lines, dancing lines. Which ones will you put in your picture today?"
>
> "Sometimes it is interesting to put different shapes together in your picture. Will you make shapes that touch or do not touch today? What shape will you make first?"
>
> "Some pictures are made with big shapes, some with little, and some with both. Will the shapes in your picture be big or little, or both?"
>
> "You can put shapes at the top of your paper, or in the middle, or at the bottom—or all over. Where do you think you will put shapes today? Where on the paper will you put the first one?"

"Do you want to turn your paper longways or sideways? What kind of a
design do you think you might make on a 'tall' paper?"
"Here are big and little pieces of paper. What kind of shapes can you make
on a little paper? On a big one? Which size of paper will you choose to
make a painting on first?"
"Here is colored paper. What colors do we have? Which will you choose to
make a painting on? What colors will you choose to paint on your
paper? Will you choose light colors or dark colors?"

BEING RESPONSIVE

During this time, as at all phases, the teacher makes a descriptive comment
that is supportive, not a value judgment. Because the child's focus is organizing lines, shapes, and colors on the paper, a teacher's comments should relate
to the issues and problems of making effective arrangements. It is helpful to
look at the children's paintings with them and to listen carefully to what they
have to say. While there is a temptation to look for subject matter in paintings
by young children, it is wise to resist this temptation and to focus instead on
the child's use of visual-graphic elements. When children are involved in
organizing lines, shapes, and colors, it is confusing and even deflating to them
to suggest that they might or should be making representational paintings.

To support the child an adult can comment about the visual-graphic
elements and their arrangement. For example, a teacher might say to Libby,
4:5 (Figure 9), "You made some rectangles. Which is the biggest? The
smallest? The tallest?" Or in responding to James, 5:10 (Figure 11), a teacher
might say, "You made two dark shapes that just touch each other. One is at the
top of your picture, and one is at the bottom. They both look like they are
moving. Can you show how they are moving with your hand?"

If a child asks, "Do you like my picture?" the answer "Yes" can include
some specific reasons such as, "I like the way you choose a dark color to paint
the numbers in your picture (cf. Figure 12; Sally, grade 1). They really stand
out against the white shape behind them."

Other comments might include some similar to the following.

"Where are all the places that you put this yellow in your picture? Did you
make any other yellowish colors?"
"You put a big shape here and little shapes over on the other side. The way
you arranged the shapes makes my eyes look at all of your painting."
"You made three different kinds of lines in your picture. Can you remember how you made each one? Where did you make the lines
touch? Where are they side-by-side?"

It may be easier for teachers to frame a comment if they look for
repetition and variation in the visual-graphic elements. In addition the
arrangement of the elements may create symmetrical patterns and regular or
irregular rhythms suitable for comment. This is a very good moment to think

with the child about the parts of the design and how they fit into the shape of the whole paper. It is important not to impose adult concepts on the child and to attempt to see these designs from the perspective of the child who painted them. If adults remember to look for relationships between the elements such as same-different, together-apart, big-little, and inside-outside, they will be relatively in tune with the children.

When a child is just finishing, it is excellent to ask, "Is it just the way you want it?" This question helps the child to review the painting and to make whatever adjustments may seem necessary without in any way suggesting that additions are needed. It is also appropriate at this time for children to learn the good work habit of standing back to reflect on their work. Acquiring this habit provides a good foundation for self-evaluation and thoughtful attention to craft.

ORDER MAKING AND EVALUATION

Even though the design quality of children's work is at a high point there will be considerable variation in the body of work done by an individual child. This is likely to include some finished designs with less or more elaboration, as well as some false starts, failed attempts, and experiments with new ideas. In order to be able to get a good idea of a child's progress, it is well to establish a rule that the children may not throw their work away without first consulting the teacher. As children become more self-critical, they become more likely to discard their work, and often the work they want to throw away is most revealing of their thought.

Many children develop a particular style or type of design, which they continue to work within for some time. It is helpful if the teacher becomes familiar with this style and can offer questions to help the child refine and extend it. These kinds of paintings should not be thought of as repetitious, but rather as evidence that the child understands it is possible to create variations within a set of self-imposed limits.

Part III
FIRST REPRESENTATIONS

5 Names for Configurations and Symbols from Designs

AGES 2, 3, 4, 5

NEW UNDERSTANDINGS ABOUT PAINTING

Children begin to discover the depictive possibilities of drawing and painting when they begin to notice images in nonrepresentational configurations they have already made. A child may discover that very motoric zigzags share their linear movement, orientation, and numerosity with objects such as grass, teeth, or spider's legs (cf. Plate IV; Merry, 3:6). Scatterings of dots may be seen as rain, tears, or "lots of candies." Much as adults see images in clouds, children begin to see similarities between real world objects and the marks they have drawn.

The capacity to represent or symbolize experience is part of human nature and begins to emerge more and more strongly during the second year. Children begin to exercise this inherent human trait first in making imitative gestures and then in language. A short time later in symbolic play, children use objects and gestures to recreate familiar experiences. For example, a child of two may place several small blocks on a larger block and call them "cookies on a plate." However, it takes longer for children to begin to make graphic representations. This is probably because they must first learn tool use itself and then to control the medium, a particularly difficult task with paint. Probably for this reason as well, they name configurations only off and on during the second and third year and slowly begin to make representations consistently toward the end of that period.

In this later period of transition children often shift from designing to representing in the middle of a painting. One is sometimes fortunate enough to be watching as this happens, thus, gaining insight into the child's thought processes.

In the painting of the spider (Plate IV) Merry, 3:6, began near the center of the paper with a full brush of paint but as she expanded her arm movements into looping, angled zigzags, the paint began to run out and the drier brush made light, airy lines. At this point the teacher heard Merry say to herself, "Charlotte's web, I'm making the spider and everything." Once the feathery lines had suggested either the web or the legs of the famous story-book spider to her, Merry went on with the image. She rounded and filled in the center with blue to give Charlotte a more substantial body; then she added the blue zigzag to the right and many blue dots below it. Since Charlotte's babies figure importantly in the story and mothers and babies are an important theme for young children, these are probably the many spider babies. But now Charlotte and her children were the same color and Merry returned to change the color of Charlotte's body by painting red over the blue to make it more distinct. Merry had continued with a planned image once the theme had been sug-

gested, by representing the substance of the larger body with a larger patch of distinct color and the size and numerousness of the children with many dots. She had used a few simple but expressive means as representational cues.

In another example (Figure 13) Kate, 4:8, had been making shapes with at least one perpendicular angle. In the course of her exploration of perpendiculars, she painted a square in the lower center of the paper and divided it with crossed lines. It suddenly occurred to her that this last configuration was like a window. Once she had discovered its "windowishness," Kate added a dot of red paint in each quadrant to represent the panes of glass. This configuration of rectangles (without the dots) will come, in time, to be a standard component of most children's paintings of houses.

It is commonly thought that a representation is an attempt to reproduce the image that enters the eye, but this is a misunderstanding. It would be closer to the truth to say that graphic representation is a process of selecting from our visual and nonvisual knowledge significant features of objects and making a match between these and the visual-graphic properties of the materials we are working with. This selecting and matching of properties is very apparent in children's early representations because they use many fewer clues than adults and also because the clues they use are very simple.

These clues are based on properties such as spatial arrangements of inside and outside, touching and not touching (Piaget and Inhelder 1956).

In Figure 14 (Josh, 5:2) the child probably began a design in which many different lines and patches are contained inside a large, red, enclosing line. When he had finished Josh said, "This is a machine; these are sparks," pointing to lines at the left, "and these are hooks," pointing to lines at the right. He had used enclosure and

numerosity as representational clues to define the machine as a container of many parts—at least in visual terms. In addition he used size, since the parts were smaller than the containing enclosure and diagonal line orientation and perpendicular angles in the "hooks."

Shapes may or may not be used. Often, lines or dots are considered sufficient. When shape is used, it is generally either an irregular patch or a

Figure 13. Configuration Named "Window." Kate, 4:8.

Figure 14. Machine with Sparks at the Left and Hooks at the Right. Josh, 5:2.

Figure 15.   A Person.   Sarah, 3:10.

geometric form. Contoured shapes appear very rarely and are generally discovered accidentally rather than produced deliberately.

In addition to these properties, children also use a variety of expressive, physiognomic properties (Werner 1948; Werner and Kaplan 1963). This set of properties is based on our natural ability to respond to the movement in lines and shapes and to the emotional qualities of lines, shapes, and colors, for example, the ominous, heavy feeling conveyed by the large dark shape, or the light, wiggling quality conveyed by the leg-web lines in Merry's painting (Plate IV). Young children are very responsive to these properties and many of their first namings (as well as later preplanned paintings) use expressive properties as representational clues. These are often hard for adults to recognize without help, but once the symbol is explained the basis of the representation usually becomes clear.

Since shape is often omitted and representational clues are fewer, it is often helpful to try to engage the child in conversation before deciding whether a representation is intended or not. This can be done by commenting on the lines, shapes, or colors, as suggested earlier, since these comments do not assume that the child has or has not intended an image. It is particularly helpful to listen to the children's own comments at this time, for we discover all too often what we thought a design is a representation and what we thought a representation is a design.

Children's early intentional symbols are often modifications or combinations of designs they have been making for some time. Many of their early designs are relatively simple combinations of lines and geometric shapes, and these are easy to adapt into representations as Kate's window (Figure 13) demonstrates. One of the earliest and most common types of symbol is the configuration for a person derived from the design of a circle with radiating

Figure 16.   An Airplane and Its Runway.   Zack, 4:6.

lines (cf. Figure 15; Sarah, 3:10). In their prior experiments with circles children devise a variety of ways to embellish the circle's powerful edge. A favorite technique for this is placing perpendicular lines along the perimeter. It is easy for the children to do this because the 90 degree angle is the first and most preferred angle of children. The resulting design is compelling to them because the circle with radiating lines simultaneously centers and dazzles the eye. Children often modify it by adding elements within the circumference and sometimes name the result "a spider" or "daddy long-legs." To convert this configuration to a person, the child retains the circle as a representation of the mass of a figure, adding simple features to indicate a face. Finally, the child selects from among the radiating lines a sufficient number to indicate that the mass of the body has projections or appendages attached to it. Often two will do for this, as in Sarah's painting, seemingly representing both arms and legs. Thus, design knowledge makes it possible to create a planned symbol.

In time children come to choose and represent objects more on the basis of their thoughts about them than on the basis of designs they know, though they still use expressive properties as representational clues.

For example, Zack, 4:6 (Figure 16), chose to represent an airplane. He painted it as a large oblong with lines projecting perpendicularly from its sides (the wings), many circles within the oblong (many windows), and a set of wheels in front of each wing. He was not concerned with the shape of the body, except that it is large and oblong, nor with that of the wings, except that these two shapes are oriented in relation to the body and project sharply. The windows are indicated simply by their number, enclosure, and location. The wheels are placed on the basis of their proximity to the wings and location outside the body of the plane. To the left, represented by its color and expanse of surface is the runway. Zack selected these characteristics and laid them out in the most convenient graphic manner on the flat paper. His use of large patches to stand for large entities, of sharply angled projections, of numerosity, and of spatial relations based on enclosure, separation, and proximity is characteristic of early planned representations.

Most early planned representations are of single objects on an otherwise blank paper surface. It may be that including anything other than the object is too difficult at first. However, children occasionally add a bit of road directly under the wheels of a car to indicate the surface upon which the automobile moves. Zack painted a large black runway beside his plane thereby including in the picture the road that makes it possible for the plane to take off and get into motion.

Children's fascination with motion expands at this time to include fascination with representation of things that move. The influence of movement on painting that began with children's delight in motoric activity with paint has come to include use of the appearance of movement in lines and shapes for representation. This influence now begins to appear as a particular interest in moving objects as subject matter. Thus, vehicles are a favorite theme, and the means by which they move, the machinery and wheels, favorite attributes. This interest in movement also causes frequent depiction of stairs and smoke (the moving breath of a house) in representations of houses.

A painting of a truck (Figure 17; Sam, 4:1) is a good example of young children's interest in vehicles, machinery, and moving parts.

Sam began by painting a red line along the bottom of the truck from left to right, beginning with the front fender and ending with the right fender. He added the rear tire in red and then began to mix brown on his tray. With this he made the center of the front wheel and then a large circular enclosure from the top of the front fender to the top of the rear fender. With a right angle he depicted the attachment of the rear wheel to the truck. Then he painted the rectangle at the left for the hood and added the "machinery" inside it, including the steering wheel. Then he made another wheel and connections in the upper right. Darkening the color, he painted the interior, perhaps a window and seats, and then reinforced the front and rear wheels with black. Finally, he painted the driver, using a circular head and stick body. He added an extra stroke (arms) below the chin to make sure the driver was touching the steering wheel. Sam's painting emphasizes the wheels, their attachment to the truck, and the steering machinery of the truck.

GETTING STARTED

As in the previous phases, the materials themselves and the teacher's presence, interest, and basic support are enough motivation for some children. However, a brief question is helpful to many children. An open-ended

Plate I. Color Mixing: Red, Yellow, Blue, Black, and White. Rod, 3:1.

Plate II. Painting with Three Ideas. Billy, 3:6.

Plate III. Design with Shapes, Textures, and Overpainting. Alan, grade 1.

Plate IV. Charlotte's Web the Spider and Everything. Merry, 3:6.

Plate V. In the Jungle. Stuart, 5:10.

Plate VI.   Me and My Friend Riding Horses.   Alex, grade 2.

Plate VII.   Eskimos Getting Up in the Morning.   Joey, grade 4.

Plate VIII. The Wolf's Den.   Jill, grade 6.

Plate IX. Cooking.   Elizabeth, grade 6.

Figure 17. Truck and Driver. Sam, 4:1.

question posed in a way that allows each child in the group the choice of making a representational or nonrepresentational picture is best at this time. Questions can refer to shapes, lines, or colors, and children can choose to use them either to make designs or representations. Some helpful questions might include the following.

"What kinds of lines do you know how to make? Do you want to use them to make a design or to make a picture of something that you know?"

"Circles are good shapes to make things with. You can make all kinds, big ones and little ones; use many colors or few colors; make them touching or apart. Do you want to use them to make a picture of a thing or a design?"

"Which color do you especially like? How can you use it in a picture?" (e.g., "green in a design or for grass," "red to make pink or to make a fire.")

"Yesterday you made a design with a house in it. What will you paint today?"

Later on, questions can refer to different basic kinds of symbols, how they are made, and the possibility of using the symbol alone or in a design. Here are some examples.

"You have been making a lot of people. Will you try to make a person today?" Then, "What shape will you use for the body? What else will it have?"

"You like cars; do you want a car in your picture? What shape will you use for a car? What parts do you want to add?"

"Do you want to make a person or an animal? What shapes will you use? Do you want to make some parts of your picture a design and some parts a story?"

"You Have to Show Me How"

From an early age on children ask adults to draw for them. If they are toddlers, this often is simply an invitation to join in the activity so that the child can enjoy it with an adult. In these cases the paper can be shared, and the partners take turns drawing, as in a spoken dialogue. Adults participating in such an activity should take care to paint or draw as the child is doing, to avoid overwhelming the child, just as they would if in conversation. Under these circumstances a pictorial sharing session can be most supportive of the child's own thoughts and abilities.

Later, however, there are more apt to be occasions when a child wants to make a particular object very much but cannot imagine how to do so. This situation requires a different strategy. The adult should first discuss the characteristics of the object or event the child is interested in, making sure the child has a good idea of its distinguishing characteristics. If not, some research is needed in pictures or other resource material, which can be put aside for occasional reference as the child begins to work. Once the child has selected the important features, the adult can help by asking how they might be made in the painting, helping the child to determine possible means of representation. A question establishing a good place to begin is helpful too. Often this is sufficient to get the child under way, but there are some occasions when a child needs more help, as the following account of an actual classroom incident reveals.

Tom, 4:4 (Figure 18), entered the classroom, marched eagerly up to the teacher and announced, "I have to make a giraffe and you have to show me how." The teacher asked where he had last seen a giraffe and what it looked like. After hearing that Tom had a pretty good idea of long legs, long neck, and small head, the teacher suggested that he begin. He refused and insisted that the teacher show him how to make a giraffe.

Then the teacher said, "All right, I'll stay here and we'll do it together. What shall we begin with, the head or the body?"

Tom: "The body." He waited.

Teacher: "Good, make the body."

Tom: "Where?"

Teacher: "Right where it belongs on the paper."

Tom: "Oh." He painted the large body circle in red and then filled it with green he had made by mixing blue and yellow. Then he said, "Now what shall I make?"

Teacher: "Shall we make the legs or the neck next?"

Tom: "The legs." He waited.

Teacher: "Good, make the legs."

Tom: "Where?"

Teacher: "Right where they belong, touching the body."

Tom: "Oh." He painted the right leg with red, then painted it over with blue and painted the other legs directly in blue. Then he said, "What shall I do next?"

Teacher: "Do you want to paint the head or the neck next?"

Tom: "The neck." He waited.

Teacher: "Good, paint the neck."

Tom: "Where?"

Teacher: "Right where it belongs, touching the body."

Tom: "Oh." He painted the neck with

mixed red and black and then asked, "What shall I do next?"

Teacher: "Well, the head is left to do."

Tom: "Oh, where shall I put it?"

Teacher: "Right where it belongs, touching the paint at the end of the neck."

Tom: "Oh." He painted the head in grey made from black and white and then exclaimed, "I made a giraffe! I made a giraffe! Now I know what I am going to do." He then added four dark and one lighter decorative zigzags with no need for discussion.

There are two general principles to be gleaned from the story of Tom and his painting of a giraffe. First, it is important to stay with a child such as Tom, who wants intensely to do something but who does not know how to do it. Such children are uncertain and afraid of their inability; at the same time their need to succeed is at its height. There is some reason, often unknown, that is investing the making of this particular picture with great importance for the child. In this circumstance the supportive presence of an adult helps greatly to give children the courage to leap into the unknown and try the task. Second, children are greatly assisted if the adult takes the problem apart and breaks it up into logical and possible chunks for them—but does not provide solutions. In painting any object it is necessary to determine the parts to be represented and the sequence in which to paint them. The analysis of parts and sequence is a difficult mental task for young children. As was evident in Tom's case, assistance with this analysis was of great help to him, without in any way dictating the form the image would take.

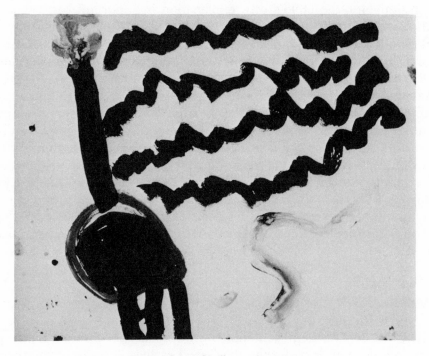

Figure 18.   A Giraffe.   Tom, 4:4.

This principle holds true for children of all ages. Children's images get richer and their means of representation more complex, but once the teacher is reasonably clear about what the child wishes to accomplish (this is not always easy to figure out), it is usually possible to *take the problem apart* and present it in pieces so that the child's success is reasonably assured.

It should be clear that this technique avoids the danger of offering children images based on adult thinking that they may admire but have not yet developed the cognitive capacity to understand. This is the case, for example, when elementary school children are taught perspective. Some can reproduce it by rote, but their inconsistent use of it makes clear they do not understand it. It also causes their paintings to lack unity, which is destructive to the aesthetic quality of their compositions.

BEING RESPONSIVE

Looking closely at their paintings with the children will help the teacher and the children to see how they have used lines and shapes to represent experience. This can be done individually or in groups. Attention in itself will support the individual child and often prompt comments such as, "Look, I made a man." To this, the teacher could respond, helping to verbalize and bring the process into focus, "Yes, you used a big circle for his body and lines for his arms and legs." A descriptive comment draws the child's attention to the process used and thus encourages growth.

Waiting for the child's own explanation is important because simple symbols can mean different things to the child. Also, a painting may have one symbol with many additional lines and shapes added for design purposes (cf. Figure 18). It is therefore unwise and may even be confusing to the child to ask, "What is this?" about lines and shapes that for the child have no representational meaning. However, there are supportive ways to encourage a child to talk about a painting. Often, an adult simply looking carefully at the painting will elicit an explanation. The question, "Do you want to tell me about your picture?" may encourage a child to explain the intention. Then if, for example, a child says, "This is a girl in the rain," a response could be, "When were you out in the rain? Was it raining hard? You made a lot of raindrops." This asks the child to recall the real-life experience and to notice the synthesis of it in the painting. A teacher might ask Zack (Figure 16) "When did you see an airplane? Did it take off? How would the plane in your picture take off?"

ORDER MAKING AND EVALUATION

With the discovery of representation there often occurs a temporary drop off of the fine skills of organization developed earlier. Portions of the painting may be as skillful and as expressive as the child's earlier work, while others are unfinished or smeared and crudely drawn. Organization of the whole may be lost as some portions of the painting take on representational meaning. Often the paper has a transitory or sketchbook quality as the child passes through designing, discovering, representation, and back to designing. There may be a single configuration or several scattered more or less at random over the paper; sometimes the child paints symbol onto symbol, onto symbol, in undifferentiated over-paintings. The smoke becomes the fire, becomes the clouds, becomes the water, becomes the grass, as the colors and lines change. The painting is the record of a series of thoughts with paint, the record of a process. This process differs from that of the first phase in that this is a process of changing thoughts about imagery while earlier it was a repetition of movements. Understanding the need for unfinished and less ordered work at this time enables the teacher to see and support the growth inherent in it.

Some children seem to enjoy painting representationally while others prefer making designs, and most children occasionally make combinations of both. They begin to make representations at a wide variety of ages, depending on their previous experience and personal preference. Children should not be urged, nor delayed, from making representations, but allowed to grow naturally into this next phase of painting. They can be discouraged both by being pushed and by being ignored. For these reasons it is particularly important in evaluating not to assume representational ability at any fixed age as a necessary sign of development. Rather, it is important to follow each child's work looking for increasing depth and richness. It is equally important to accept intervals of disinterest and to be alert for the period of disorder that often precedes major steps forward in development. Finally, when children begin to represent, it is important to discover their intentions and study their methods of making images in order to be supportive in this phase of expression that is difficult for us to understand.

Part IV
PICTURING EXPERIENCE

6 Simple Images: People, Houses, Animals

AGES 5, 6, 7

NEW UNDERSTANDINGS ABOUT PAINTING

Children's capacity to think logically develops rapidly between the ages of five and seven (Piaget and Inhelder 1969). These new logical skills—especially the ability to group items into sets or classes has a marked effect on children's graphic symbols. Earlier, symbols were often based on strong sensory impressions. (For example, the way in which the overall quality of "roundishness" is a basis for the painting of spiders in Plate IV, machinery in Figure 14, or a person in Figure 15.) The sensory impressions children used were frequently charged with personal emotions and quite idiosyncratic. By contrast, later symbols take into account how items are conceptually similar to and different from others, as children make more objective appraisals of them. Younger children of this period often make symbols of "an animal" in which the basic features of the class are depicted, such as walking on all fours. Later they will add the attributes of particular species in the class and represent a cat by adding ears, tail, and whiskers to the basic symbol for animal.

Symbols of Basic Categories

While paintings are still often developed from designs (cf. Figure 19; Kevin, grade 1) the influence of these new logical abilities is evident. It first appears when children begin to depict basic types of objects; that is, the symbols in their paintings represent the largest possible class to which each object might belong. They paint symbols of "persons" without any graphic indications for sex or age (cf. Figure 20; Bobby, grade 1), animals of no particular species (cf. Plate V; Stuart, 5:10), and houses of no specific design (cf. Figure 21; Tim, grade 1).

Children repeat their basic category symbols many times, gaining control and competence at representing experiences. In time they start to include more information in their representations and to paint more specific subcategory symbols, such as the girl depicted with long hair and a skirt in "Me

57

Figure 19.   A Dinosaur.   Kevin, grade 1.

Figure 20.   My Father Took Us to the Zoo.   Bobby, grade 1.

Figure 21. Me Upstairs in Bed. Tim, grade 1.

and My Brother Walking My Dog" (Figure 22; Melanie, grade 2); "The Town Library" (Figure 23; Todd, grade 1) with its clock and tower, painted after a class trip; or the horses with soft pink muzzles and elongated heads in "Me and My Friend Riding Horses" (Plate VI; Alex, grade 2).

A child's choice of which attributes or details to include depends on two factors. First, the choice rests on which attributes the child considers to be necessary. This may include basic parts such as head, body, legs, ears, eyes, tail, but also parts with personal meaning such as the pink noses on Alex's horses (Plate VI). Second, the choice rests on which attributes lend themselves most easily to representation within the child's graphic means.

Representation

The task of representation is to select and match up characteristics of experience with characteristics of the medium. We must balance ideas about objects and knowledge of the material in the decision making process, using both visual and nonvisual knowledge (Werner and Kaplan 1963). Children in this phase work out the match by determining the essential parts of an object, relating them to the basic graphic elements they have learned (circle, rectangle, line, and dot), and assembling whole symbols by joining these elements

Figure 22.   Me and My Brother Walking My Dog.   Melanie, grade 2.

Figure 23.   The Town Library.   Todd, grade 1.

where the parts of the object touch each other. Here is an observation of a six-year-old boy forming symbols in this way.

In a group discussion of activities the children had enjoyed over the weekend, Bobby, grade 1 (Figure 20) decided to paint about a trip to the zoo with his father and brother. First, he painted a basic category symbol of an animal, added a trunk transforming it into an elephant, and then he painted a cage over it, all in blue. Then he used red to make the animal in a cage to the left and the basic category symbols for "persons" at the bottom of the paper. He said the figure on the right was his father. By the time he painted his father, there was not much space left and he was getting tired.

In his painting Bobby used circles for the heads and rectangles for the bodies. He oriented the person symbols vertically and one animal symbol horizontally. Most animals are painted horizontally. (The small animal in the cage to the left is probably oriented vertically because there was not enough space to paint in a cage horizontally.) Bobby used lines for limbs and dots for eyes. He did not use color representationally but simply chose colors he liked.

As Bobby's painting shows, relating the object to the medium depends on the child's knowledge of the medium. It also depends on the processes of perception. Perception selects out the structure in a visual scene and distills the essences of forms (Arnheim 1974). For example, using this kind of visual analysis, children understand heads as round and limbs as narrow. Matching these perceptual concepts to the graphic concepts of circularity and linearity, children use circles to stand for heads, lines to stand for arms and legs. Different types of matches enter the child's repertoire as the child's capacity to entertain more complex thoughts grows. Among the properties three- and four-year-olds use to make matches are number, enclosure, and physiognomic expressive qualities. They frequently omit shape. Unlike these younger children, five-, six-, and seven-year-olds regularly use shape. However, they do not regularly use color as a property upon which to build matches. In the next phase color will be incorporated as a representational feature.

It is important to point out that the matching process also depends on the child's intentions. Children can now distinguish between schematic imagery being used for economy (e.g., the audience in "The Horse Show at Madison Square Garden" [Figure 24]), decorative embellishment (e.g., the colors and texture in "The Jungle" [Plate V]), an emphasis on design (e.g., "The Dinosaur" [Figure 19]), and the descriptive symbols useful in a straight narrative. They select and often combine these different modes of painting according to their intention.

Another factor that influences the depictions children make is their need to distinguish the symbol for one category clearly from another. The symbols for people and animals are similar, but children differentiate them by drawing animals horizontally and adding tails or ears. Cars and houses have doors and windows, are rectangular, and often have people in them. But cars have wheels and houses have chimneys; thus, children include them.

Space

It does not occur to children of this age to conform to the convention that images should be made from a single point of view. Thus, they are able to select the most graphically convenient and telling aspects of objects and to combine them freely. In the painting of "The Horse Show at Madison Square Garden" (Figure 24; John, grade 2) the exterior facade of the building is simply joined at the top with an aerial view of the interior. The front view of the facade and the aerial view of the ring are chosen for convenience, since these are the easiest aspects to translate into the circles and rectangles of the child's graphic vocabulary. (The horse may be seen on the right in the ring, preparing to take the jump at the left.)

It is probably inaccurate to label young children's symbols as top, side, or front "views" since the child is not, in fact, selecting a viewpoint or spatial position from which to represent the object or scene. What *is* being selected is the side, face, aspect, or position of individual objects that lends itself most conveniently to translation into the child's graphic language (Arnheim 1974), as in the interior and exterior of Madison Square Garden, or the noses attached at the sides of the faces of the two horseback riders (cf. Plate VI; Alex, grade 2). Children of these ages are adroit in selecting a revealing aspect of an object, becoming more and more conscious of the significance these choices play in creating imagery.

Figure 24. The Horse Show at Madison Square Garden.   John, grade 2.

Once a convenient aspect is chosen, it may be joined with other convenient aspects wherever they touch or located above, below, or to the side of others. Elements may also be placed inside or outside of other elements. This latter system dominates the spatial organization in "The Jungle" (Plate V; Stuart, 5:10), for example. These are the same spatial concepts (together/ apart, inside/outside) observed in the beginning phase of representation. Since children have no rule requiring consistent use of aspects, it is easy for them to organize paintings using these spatial concepts.

Overlapping is rarely used at this age. When it is present, as in the painting "My Father Took Us to the Zoo" (Figure 20; Bobby, grade 1), it is necessary to the event being depicted, *not* an indication of the painter's point of view. Children depict the bars over the animals in cages at an early age, motivated by the need to make it clear that the animals are safely restrained.

Representation of environmental space surrounding objects develops more slowly. In the first phase of representation, from two to five years, children think of the paper as a blank surface waiting to receive the depiction of one object (or several separate objects) as on a sketchbook page. Even though they have developed the ability to organize a whole paper surface when making designs, they have not yet begun to think of the paper as an equivalent for a unit of real space. They sometimes represent two objects in relation to each other as was the case in the "Airplane and Runway" (Figure 16; Zack, 4:6) and "Truck and Driver" (Figure 17; Sam 4:1), but it does not occur to them to depict the surrounding environmental space.

In this later phase children begin the arrangement of symbols in a coherent space. The children begin to conceive of the whole paper as an environment and to relate figures to each other in this space. Relying on their topological concepts of space, children sometimes use circular shapes as representations of enclosing shapes as Stuart, 5:10, does when he uses an enclosure to contain figures in "The Jungle" (Plate V). More often children use another very simple form of spatial organization—they align objects on the two basic axes of the paper. Objects that rest on the earth are located along a line at the base (cf. Figure 22; Melanie, grade 2) or sometimes objects are placed on the bottom edge of the paper itself (cf. Figure 23; Todd, grade 1). Objects that are tall or objects that are located further back in space are simply located higher on the paper. Sometimes there is a skyline. The result of this is often a rather stiff placement of symbols along the baseline, a large band of "air" in the middle, with a strip of sky at the top. The center portion is often left as a void unless some aspect of the narrative requires the inclusion of an object.

This area in the center of the paper gradually takes on meaning as the objects and events children wish to portray require imagery in the middle of the paper. The use of the upper portion of the paper for the ring at Madison Square Garden (Figure 24; John, grade 2) is one such image. In another, "Me Upstairs in Bed" (Figure 21; Tim, grade 1), the painter was obliged to make the house extend up the paper for two reasons. He wanted to include the information that his bedroom was on the second floor of the house. Also, he had to make a room large enough to hold a horizontal image of a person. These extensions of imagery into the upper portions of the paper depend on the demands of the narrative. In time they cause children to conceive of the paper as a whole unit of space.

The kind of representation Tim used for his house has been called "x-ray" because the viewer is presumed to be seeing through the front wall of the house. However, since children are not yet painting representations based on a single point of view, they are probably not making "x-ray" images at all. Instead, the outline of the house may be thought of as standing for its inside and outside simultaneously.

As children grow, their awareness of the inherent conflict between the flatness of the paper and the three-dimensionality of experience increases. Most children cannot use perspective to devise a resolution to this conflict until well into high school. However, until the fourth or fifth grade, children whose unique representations of space have been accepted by adults and who have been encouraged to value their own imagery, invent many ways to represent space that are communicative and expressive. Such children remain confident and able to depict their experiences.

Themes and the Motivation for Growth

In this phase children select a subject ahead of time on the basis of interest rather than by reading symbolic meaning into a graphic configuration. Their interests are focused primarily on themselves, so most themes include the painter, painter's family, toys, pets, and everyday activities such as "Me and My Brother Walking My Dog" (Figure 22; Melanie, grade 2) or "Me Upstairs in Bed" (Figure 21; Tim, grade 1). Familiar places, close to home or school provide most settings. Fears and aggressions may be expressed unconsciously in subjects such as "The Dinosaur" (Figure 19; Kevin, grade 1) or "The Jungle" (Plate V; Stuart, 5:10). Fantasies of power, fame, and beauty appear in portraits of heroes and heroines such as baseball players or princesses. In spite of their relatively narrow range of themes and simple graphic means, young children have a remarkable ability to capture complex human emotions and situations in their paintings as "Me Upstairs in Bed" (Figure 21; Tim, grade 1) exemplifies.

Together with their developing cognitive abilities, children's growing social abilities make it possible for them to form more relationships, to travel further from home, and to engage in a wider variety of activities. This range of activities, continually expanding with the children's inherent eagerness for new experiences, adds more and more to their range of themes as they grow.

In addition, becoming increasingly aware of their individuality and difference from others, they discover the communicative aspect of art. Until now they have taken for granted that their work would be understood and welcomed. With increased social awareness they begin to wonder if others recognize their intentions and to strive for communicative images.

Indeed, in these years the motivating force behind the growth of children's imagery is their need to "tell the story." Because this need to formulate and communicate is so strong and because the range of their experiences is expanding, they are continually obliged to invent new means of representation. Thus, the mainspring behind children's growth in painting for the next several years is their own need to recreate experiences in visual form. The vigor of their energetic and thoughtful efforts to get all the important parts of "the story" into the painting testifies to the satisfaction they derive from creating meaning in paintings.

In sum this phase, with its basic and subcategory symbols and its baseline environments, marks a significant change in what it is possible for children to represent and how it is possible for them to devise representations. This is made possible by a dramatic change in children's capacity to organize their knowledge about objects and events and to use visual-graphic means systematically for representation. Changes in their paintings also reflect children's growing awareness of the need to insure that images communicate and of their expanding range of experiences.

GETTING STARTED

Good art expresses the deeply personal thoughts and feelings of the artist. Art based on the ideas or emotions of another is often derivative and lacks honesty and power. But art is not created in a vacuum. The source of artistic expression is the life experiences of the artist.

This is just as true for children as adults. Thus, it is important that subject matter for paintings be from the life experiences of children (not adults) and from the personal experience of each individual child (Dewey 1902). To insure each child's involvement and success, teachers need to awaken and engage each child's ideas and feelings about experiences as a motivating force. Children's urge to capture experience is strong, but it depends on their interest in the subject being depicted.

For these reasons it is important to make it possible for each child to reflect on events that are immediate and personally meaningful. A short discussion initiated around an age-appropriate, but general, theme allows each individual to search his or her memory for a meaningful personal event related to the theme. For example, a teacher might ask, "What is your favorite new toy?" Thereafter, in order to help each child find an individual subject, a teacher can ask several times, "Who has a different idea?" The discussion should help each child to identify an important experience and then go on to bring into awareness important aspects of the experience. Such questions as "Why do you like it? How do you play with it? Where do you play with it?" can be asked of several children. Their answers will help the others to develop their own ideas without necessarily having to speak.

In addition a few minutes spent planning how to translate their "idea" into paint helps the children to make rich and well-composed pictures. For example, identifying the parts and their relation to the whole is helpful. The teacher might ask, "What shapes will you use to make your new bicycle? How big will you need to paint it on the paper?" The discussion should end when most of the children appear to have an idea on their minds. They reveal this by their statements and by the expressions on their faces. A final question or two helps children to make the transition from discussion to action. The teacher can ask "What will you paint first, yourself or your bicycle? What is the very first thing you are going to paint?" This helps the children to begin to think about how to sequence their actions in order to make the experience come to life on the paper.

These dialogues between teacher and children (or one child or a small group) have three distinct parts. In the first the teacher offers a theme to the group through a topic question and helps the children to call forth important experiences and the associations with and ideas about the experience each child finds most meaningful. In the second the teacher helps the children to think about translating their chosen subjects into paint. These questions often refer to lines, shapes, colors, size, and location on the paper. In the third a few questions help the children to decide how to start their paintings.

The purpose of these discussions is to help the children focus on and review their own thoughts. Thus, most of the teacher's statements should be questions, and whatever answers the children offer should be considered appropriate. Right and wrong do not enter such a discussion, nor is it crucial that each child ultimately paint a subject he or she has discussed. Some children change their plans when they begin to work. The overall purpose of the dialogue is to get the children thinking. Individual children who arrive with an important experience on their minds should, of course, be encouraged to paint it. They do not need the suggestion of a general theme, but they do benefit from the rest of the discussion. To "I'm going to make my new dog," a teacher might reply, "What shapes will you use for its head, its body? What other parts will it have? What color will you paint it?"

To encourage the children's development of symbols, it is helpful to select themes that emphasize people, animals, houses, vehicles, and the immediate environment.

One example of a beginning dialogue follows.

"What kind of a house do you live in?"
"Is it tall?"
"Do several families live in it?"
"Is there a tree near it?"
"What special parts does it have?"
"Does it have a pointed roof?"
"What shape are the windows?"
"How will you make them with the paint?"
"Will you start with the ground or the house?"
"What is the very first thing you are going to paint?"

Another example of questions for one lesson is provided next.

"What animal do you know that is fierce, and which one do you know that is
     friendly?"
"Which do you want to paint today?"
"What kind of ears does he have?"
"Can you draw the shape they are in the air with your finger?"
"What other parts will you paint?"
"Where does the animal live?"
"How will you show that in your picture?"
"How big will you paint the animal on your paper?"
"What is the first thing you are going to paint?"

Other themes for lessons might include the following.

"Where do you play with your friend, indoors or outdoors?"
"How do you travel, in a car, plane, truck, or bus?"
"What do you like to do with your mother (or father)?"
"Where do you go away from home, to the country, to the city?"
"What do you like to do at home?"
"What do you do in your sneakers?"
"Where do you play outdoors?"
"What is your favorite game to play?"
"What do you do when it rains?"
"What is your favorite thing to do in the summer, the winter?"
"What do you like to do at school?"

Occasionally a child cannot make a strong commitment to an idea during
the discussion or lacks confidence and needs a bit of extra help after the
group begins to paint. The same sort of discussion can take place in a
one-to-one dialogue, as well. Also, many of the follow-up questions are useful
to use with individual children after they have started painting, to help them
extend their thinking and develop richer imagery.

BEING RESPONSIVE

As the teacher pauses to look at children's work, they often offer thoughts
uppermost in their minds. If so, the adult should be sure to respond to the
concerns of the child. If a child says, "This is my new puppy," the teacher
might reply, "Oh, you must be so happy." And continue, "Is it very little?
When did you get it?" If the child does not initiate a conversation, the teacher
can ask if the child wishes to discuss the work and go on to mention the way
the child used lines and shapes to make the image. For example a teacher
might say to Melanie, grade 2 (Figure 22), "Look how you used a triangle to
make yourself and your dress and dark rectangles to make your brother's
body and pants' legs. That was very thoughtful. It was a good idea to paint

clouds up in the sky too." The description of the parts and their translation into paint helps to validate the child's effort and intention and frequently prompts the child to think of others to add, on this occasion or in the next painting (e.g., more parts of the body, clothes, or more sky).

At times a tactful question while a child is working will inspire the child to make a more complete picture. For example: "Where is your car going? Is it on a road?" or "Are you going to put yourself in your picture?" or "What else is near the school building?" Most of these questions encourage the child to make representations of people, to develop richer imagery, to unify the composition. A sparse or ineffectual painting is the sign of a child with few ideas or an insecure child. This child can often be helped by a few well-chosen questions, but children should not be directed to add specific parts. When all the children are having difficulty, it is usually the fault of the original discussion. Either the theme was not very meaningful to the children, or the discussion was not successful in helping the children to get in touch with their own thoughts and feelings. The surest way to insure strong paintings is a good discussion with the group, before the children begin.

Other responses that are helpful are directed at the combination of symbols and at the composition. A comment on several symbols in a painting will encourage children to try more combinations in the future. An adult might say to John, grade 2 (Figure 24), "It was a good idea to show the front of Madison Square Garden at the bottom of your paper and the ring at the top. The way you painted color all around the ring helps to hold the picture together. It is nice to see all the people around the ring watching, too." Or a teacher might say to Tim, grade 1 (Figure 21), "It was good that you painted the house up to the top of the paper. It shows how high you are when you are upstairs. The trees down below help to show it too. Do you feel cozy upstairs in bed at home?" Or a teacher might say to Stuart, 5:10 (Plate V), "You made a lot of different things in your painting—people, animals, and cars. I especially like the way you repeated red, pink, and orange and little lines and textures all over your picture. These help to make it into a whole picture."

If the custom is established that the children show their paintings to the teacher as they are finishing, it is possible to ask, "Is it just the way you want it?" and to use the opportunity to review the work. It is also helpful to put up the children's work from time to time and point out the different techniques children have used. One might say to a group of children, "Let us look at all the different buildings the children painted today. How are they the same and how are they different?" This helps to support the individual differences of the children and to suggest alternative methods of representation to them.

ORDER MAKING AND EVALUATION

During this period children paint designs, imagery mixed with design, and narrative pictures. The narrative pictures are sometimes individual symbols, sometimes sketchbooklike pages of unrelated symbols, and sometimes symbols combined in an environment. The three aesthetic strands of painting, narration, emotion, and composition (see Chapter 1), do not receive equal attention at this time. Children are just learning to create representational paintings and focus their attention on the narrative strand. They can consider only a limited number of ideas at any one time; thus, their natural gifts for composition and emotional expression are often less evident. The simple logic that leads them to create a whole environment with a narrow ground line also puts them at a compositional disadvantage, since it is more difficult to create a unified composition in baseline paintings with their void of "air" in the middle. This shortcoming should be understood as a necessary and temporary developmental phenomenon when evaluating children's work.

However, the symbols themselves reveal children's growing skills and imagination. Since most symbols are made with simple visual-graphic elements, a teacher can easily follow the increasing assurance and flexibility with which each child uses them from painting to painting. It is true that children use the same configurations for a considerable period of time, but they vary the position and relation of each to accommodate the narrative. For example, Tim, grade 1 (Figure 21) demonstrated his representational versatility when he painted the symbol for himself horizontally and placed it in a house enclosure high above two trees. These variations show a teacher strength and growth in the child's thinking.

It is also important to look for progress in the choice of meaningful experiences and in the rich and full accounting of them. For instance, Melanie, grade 2 (Figure 22) chose an important experience, walking her dog, and added a house, tree, and clouds in the sky. She included her brother, as well.

Sometimes a child prefers to draw lines that seem to trace around the form of objects rather than substituting simple shapes for each part. Such children may be more sensitive to shape, as, for example, Alex, grade 2 (Plate VI) was when he drew the horses' heads. At other times children may be sensitive to atmosphere as Todd, grade 1 (Figure 23) was when he surrounded "The Town Library" with sensuous brushings of paint. On other occasions the expression of emotions becomes more important, as in the powerfully brushed shapes of "The Dinosaur" (Figure 19; Kevin, grade 1). Each of these sensitivities is an important aspect of art and of individual children's interests. They should receive recognition and support.

Thus, with attention to the developmental phenomena characteristic of this period and to the specific sensitivities of individual children, adults can appreciate and evaluate children's work.

7 Richer Symbols: Friends, Workers, City Streets

AGES 7, 8, 9

NEW UNDERSTANDINGS ABOUT PAINTING

Children create their most accomplished representations of experience, in the fundamental form of childhood, during these middle school years. The dominant interest of the young child—the self—is growing to include the relation of that self to society. Children become less focused on themselves (Piaget and Inhelder 1969) and more on forming relationships with others. Their paintings reflect this in the choice of subjects and in the well-established causal links between the items depicted. They depict activities with friends, such as "My Friend and I Up in a Tree" (Figure 25; Bosley, grade 3); organized sports; and the different kinds of work adults do, such as "Men Picking Cotton" (Figure 26; Matt, grade 3). Subject matter expands because children travel further from home (cf. Figure 27; Roger, grade 4) and also because they can imagine experiences encountered indirectly through books, television (cf. Figure 28; Will, grade 4), and films. They can relate the experiences of people living in other places on the earth (cf. Plate VII; Joey, grade 4) or in other times to their own and deliberately develop imaginary situations or fantasy events.

Attributes and Their Representation

Children's symbols are no longer constructed on the fewest possible attributes needed to define the subject. In their pictures people have waists (cf. Figure 29; Jane, grade 2) and joints that bend, though the opposition of arms and legs may not be accurate (cf. Figure 28; Will, grade 4). People can also be pictured from the side, and they may be shown in special poses like the firefighters with watchful heads in "Fire in the City" (Figure 30; Susan, grade 2). A whole body may even be tilted off-balance like that of the "Scuba Diver" underwater (Figure 31; Jennifer, grade 3).

Such images reveal a new way of thinking about and understanding the human frame. Instead of simply itemizing parts as children did earlier, they

(*continued on page 74*)

Figure 25.   My Friend and I Up in a Tree.
Bosley, grade 3.

Figure 26.   Men Picking Cotton.   Matt, grade 3.

Figure 27.   The Airport.   Roger, grade 4.

Figure 28.   Olympic Games — Skating.   Will, grade 4.

Figure 29. City Streets. Jane, grade 2.

Figure 30. Fire in the City. Susan, grade 2.

Figure 31. Scuba Diver.   Jennifer, grade 3.

assemble and unify the body by thinking more of movement through the skeletal structure. The change in their thinking is revealed by the variations in shapes and the connections and orientations of body parts. As a result, arms emerge from shoulders and legs from hips (cf. Figure 28), and movement begins to flow through representations of the figure (cf. Plate VII; Joey, grade 4).

However, children still do not depict the specific contours of muscles and bones under the skin, nor do they represent its three-dimensionality. Since most children's paintings are drawn from imagination, the lack of detailed contouring is primarily a problem of memory. In fact, if children are given the opportunity to draw subjects they are interested in, such as animals, from observation, their drawings show remarkable rendering of contours (Smith 1983).

Children now clothe figures. They may depict a favorite outfit, a costume that helps to identify an activity (e.g., sports uniform or a party dress), or one that indicates an occupation or nationality. The firefighters (Figure 30) are depicted in their coats, helmets, and boots, the Eskimo (Plate VII) in his parka. Also, figures may carry objects related to the narrative, for example, the women downtown shopping (Figure 29) are carrying umbrellas and pocketbooks and the firefighters a net, hose, and ladder.

Environments are equally detailed and well defined.

The Olympic skating rink (Figure 28; Will, grade 4) is portrayed with the Olympic insignia of intertwining circles and travel advertisements on its wall, as well as a full complement of spectators. Some of the spectators wave flags, some raise binoculars in front of their eyes, and some are turned to the side. The skater, depicted in three-quarter view, is in a suit of black tights and has beautifully detailed skates. The spectators are clothed in different colors. These colors are placed around the paper to make variety and unity in the composition. The spectators are arranged in horizontal rows which repeat the horizontal lines of the rink and contrast sharply with the large upright figure of the skater. The detailed account of figures and environment in this painting is very well integrated with its fine composition.

The graphic elements children use to represent the multitude of attributes are also much more varied. A younger child (Figure 29; Jane, grade 2) still uses circles and triangles for her figures, but the shapes used to depict human beings in Figures 28, 30, 31, and in Plate VII are much more complex. They are also more unified, reflecting children's growing concept of body structure. Color is now used consistently for representation; people have flesh color, buildings are grey, and sky is various shades of blue.

Space

In the representation of space children are still indifferent to the convention of perspective; nevertheless they design the whole paper as a unit of space.

In "City Streets" (Figure 29; Jane, grade 2) the artist chose an intersection as most representative of the theme during a class discussion. She then built the composition around a powerful graphic device, the cross that represents the intersecting streets. Jane located sidewalks beside the streets and buildings (identified simply by the familiar window configuration) beside the sidewalks. In doing this she used the topological principle of placing elements together where they touch, irrespective of their orientation in space. She painted the actors in the event (people, cars, and stoplights) onto the "pictorial map" of the intersection she had first created. This indirect process of painting the environment first and then overpainting the figures on it would not be possible for a younger child. To dramatize the problem of crossing the street in heavy traffic, Jane arranged the figures facing each other across the horizontal street and aligned the stoplights parallel with it to guide them. She then added the dangerous cars. One poor shopper is trapped in the intersection with four cars converging on her! The environment in this painting is not simply a setting, but rather an integral part of the idea being depicted.

Baseline to Base Plane

The depiction of objects in the distance or behind other objects, though still prompted primarily by the narrative, becomes more common. One firefighter is almost hidden behind the net he is helping to hold, while a victim appears half-visible in a window calling for help (Figure 30). A large fish swims dangerously close, in front of the legs of the scuba diver, while water swirls around them (Figure 31). The Eskimos' igloo is dwarfed by the range of the distant mountains (Plate VII). One Eskimo peeps out of the igloo entrance, body hidden by the tunnel, while the second, back turned toward the viewer, surveys the mountains and checks the fire. Children are no longer limited to the most graphically convenient aspects of objects but can represent the sides, backs, and tops of many objects.

As images expand to occupy the whole paper it may seem that the baseline has been replaced by a base plane receding into the distance. However, these areas are usually floor plans of the ground and surround objects that are depicted in elevation. Since children feel no conflict in combining different aspects, they simply supply objects with the ground necessary to support them. Trained to read images based on perspective, adults sometimes misunderstand the child's intention and attribute perspective where it does not exist (cf. Figure 26).

Sometimes, however, a child does recognize the consequences of the observer's point of view. After Joey, grade 4 (Plate VII) had painted the Eskimos, their igloo, and fire, he asked, "What color are mountains far away?" He recognized that changes in color are brought about by atmosphere and distance. After a discussion with his teacher he mixed a light purple color to indicate mountains in the hazy distance.

At this time children also recognize that objects decrease in size as they retreat into the distance.

In a painting of an airport (Figure 27) Roger, grade 4, painted the buildings of the faraway city smaller and lighter in color. He made the air traffic controllers' tower so large and close that it disappears off the top of the paper. It overlaps the plane and a portion of the distant city. He indicated figures simply (controllers in their tower and spectators on the observation roof of the adjacent building) since the main topic of the painting is the airport and waiting plane. The painting is based on a trip Roger had recently made to the controllers' tower of the airport. His memory of the trip was triggered by a discussion in class that his teacher had begun by asking the question, "Where are places that people need to wait?" The teacher had chosen this theme to bring about closer integration between figures and environment in the imagery of the children.

The three pictorial devices that appear most often at this age, reflecting some concept of the effect of a point of view, are change of color and size with distance and overlapping. These devices are still more motivated by the narrative urge than by a wish for illusionism, but they do indicate children's growing fund of knowledge. They want to present the vastness of a space, or the relation of objects in an event, and use these helpful pictorial devices.

GETTING STARTED

Now the dialogue between children and teacher can be more extensive. Children can benefit from a longer discussion and consideration of more complex issues. As outlined in Chapter 6, the first part of a discussion should be designed to help children select a subject for painting that is personally meaningful. However, the teacher's goal in choosing themes is increasingly to present children with a challenge designed to increase their ability to express themselves. For example, since children's important experiences are likely to include people in action, themes that prompt representation of the human figure are offered. A teacher might begin a lesson with one of the following questions.

> "How do you move when you play your favorite sport?"
> "What things do you like to do sitting down?"
> "When do you lean (cf. Figure 31); when do you stretch?"
> "What kinds of things do people do sitting (or standing) at tables?"
> "What activities do you do that make you bend (cf. Figure 28)?"

Another group of themes focuses on children's growing social awareness. Initial questions to start such lessons might include the following.

> "What social activities (visits, parties, holidays) do you do with your family?"
> "What entertainment events do you go to (theater, movies, sports, parades)? Who do you go with?"
> "Do you like to go out (shopping, visiting, to clubs, after school groups)? Who do you go with?"
> "What do you like to do with your best friend?"
> "Who is a person that you admire?"
> "Where do you see people in crowds?"
> "What kinds of jobs do people have outdoors (cf. Figure 26) and what kinds indoors?"
> "What kinds of jobs do people have that are dangerous and what kinds that help people (cf. Figure 30)?"

Still another set of themes is developed around the children's new found ability to represent events other than their own immediate concrete experiences. It is important that the teacher have some idea of the interests and studies of the children in order to follow their associations. For instance, one teacher, knowing that the children were studying nontechnological societies, asked, "What are the first things you do when you get up in the morning? If you lived in a different country with a different culture, what might you do?" Joey, grade 4 (Plate VII), replied, "If I were an Eskimo, the very first thing I would do would be to look out of my igloo to check the weather and then I would build a fire."

Other questions to begin discussions might include the following.

"What do you wear when you go out? If you lived in another time (place),
   what might you wear?"

"What kinds of tools do you use? What kinds of tools did people in other
   times have?"

"How did people travel in other times? How might they travel in the
   future?"

"How did people get food in other times? How do they get it now?"

"What kinds of people were important long ago? Who are important
   people now? Who might be important in the future?"

"If you could be anywhere or anytime, where and when would you choose
   to be?"

"If you could have your dream house (or room) or dream car what would it
   be like?"

Still another type of theme is designed to bring emotions into the content
of the subject matter. For example, an excellent question to put children in
touch with their softer feelings is, "What is something quiet you like to do (at
home, with a friend)?" This was the opening question that prompted Bosley,
grade 3 (Figure 25), to paint "My Friend and I Up in a Tree." The idea is
unusual and personal, and the friendship between the boys is expressively
rendered by placing them side-by-side at the convergence of the tree
branches. Other questions that may engage the feelings of children follow.

"What do you do that makes you happy? That makes you sad?"

"When do you feel safe and strong?"

"Can you tell how animals are feeling by the way they move? How about
   people?"

"When you feel dreamy, how do you sit or stand? What kinds of things are
   you thinking about?"

"Do animals have families? How do they feel about their children?"

"What is something frightening that happened to you? What is something
   brave you have done?"

"Some machines are big and powerful, some are sturdy, some are complicated, and some are delicate. What kind of a machine would you like
   to be using?"

"What is something dangerous you know how to do now that you couldn't
   do when you were little?"

Of course, each of these questions needs to be followed up by appropriate interchanges with the children to help them explore their memories and
imaginations for significant ideas and experiences. Questions seeking the
relationships between items in the narrative may be asked, such as, "What
different kinds of things do firefighters do? What things do they do together,
—with people,—with equipment?" Extending the range of the discussion by
asking "Who had a different experience," or "Who has a different idea," is
important. It is helpful to the children to ask about the spatial setting (e.g.,

where was it, indoors or outdoors, bright day or dull day, the whole space or a part, what other objects are in the space, and so forth). These help the child to remember a rich compliment of details about the setting and thus to plan a fully organized representation of the space and a whole composition.

The segment of the dialogue that discusses means of depiction and composition can be more detailed and specific, as well. The usual questions asking what shape will be painted (e.g., to represent the bent leg), how a color will be mixed (e.g., to make the brown of the parka), and which elements of the narrative are to be included (e.g., other members of the family) should be asked. But now questions having to do with relationships may be emphasized. For example, questions having to do with size, such as, "If you want to show that the controllers' tower is very close, how big will you need to make it on the paper? How big will the controllers themselves be?" Other questions will help the children to think about the most appropriate aspects of objects. "If you make the intersection looking down, how will you make the buildings, looking down, looking sideways, or some other way?" Or "Are you going to show the skater from the front or the side?"

Questions of relationship often have to do with location in space and on the paper. For example, "If you want to show the crowd watching the skater, where will you place them on the paper?" Or "How will you show the fish is very close to the scuba diver?" Or "Are the people going to be inside or outside the stores, or both?"

Still other questions are designed to help children depict specific individual objects when these are appropriate to the narrative. While discussing a child's interest in a painting of "Playing Baseball in My Yard with Friends," a teacher might ask, "What kind of trees are in your yard? How will you show them? Will your house be in the picture? How is it different? Does it have a porch?"

In themes that include human beings in action, it is helpful to have children assume positions that may be difficult for them to depict. A teacher might ask the child wanting to paint a baseball player at bat to get into the batting stance and then to sense the feeling of the pose. This appears to be more helpful to children than looking at another child posing. (While it can be beneficial for children to draw from nature, the focus of that exercise should be observation not narration, and the pose must be maintained long enough for children to satisfy their curiosity and complete the task.)

The purpose of these discussions is to help children think over what they are planning to do. Their answers should be understood as first thoughts on the question, provisional, and subject to change. Most answers simply reveal a child's thinking and can be accepted without challenge.

When children have had enough opportunity to consider their ideas, the teacher should help the children make the transition from thought to action by asking how they plan to begin. Some typical questions are: "Will you begin with the place or with the people?" and "Are you going to paint the house or the ground first?"

BEING RESPONSIVE

Opportunities for helping children increase during this phase. Children can make more productive use of suggestions offered while they work, as well as make use of responses to finished work. In general, suggestions made during the work period should be posed as questions. It is helpful to ask questions about details of settings, clothing, tools, and individual objects, since it is now much easier for children to review and select from their wealth of knowledge. However, teachers should avoid questions that challenge the techniques of representation a child has employed. For example, it is not helpful to ask if there is another way to depict a bending figure, since the child may have struggled to achieve the one in the painting and may not be able to imagine another. Children have many more options regarding the attributes or details of subject matter than they do means of representation at this time.

If children ask for help with representation, it is important for a teacher to remember that techniques of adults may not be useful. This is particularly true with regard to the representation of the third dimension on flat paper. Teachers' suggestions should be based on the techniques of children and not the convention of perspective. When children say, "I want to make it look real," they generally do not want to use perspective in their pictures. They do want a satisfying rendering, but at this age they cannot understand perspective. It is too intellectually complex for them. The teacher can usually meet a child's needs by applying the strategy of *taking the problem apart,* first discussed in Chapter 5, in relation to "The Giraffe" (Figure 18; Tom, 4:4). If a child asks, for example, "How can I make a table in my picture look real?," discussion might begin with questions like "What sort of table do you want?" "How does it fit into the story?" Possible next questions include, "Do you need to show the whole top of the table or simply the side of the top?" "What shape do you want to use for it?" "Where do you want to attach the legs, down below or at the sides?" "How many legs do you want to have showing?" These questions allow for a wide range of personal solutions to the depiction of a table, none of which depends on perspective.

Dialogues about composition are very worthwhile during the work period, reminding children to keep this aspect of the task in mind. Questions can be framed to help children disregard the narrative and focus on the relation of graphic elements in the composition. For example, a teacher may ask, "You used a rectangle for the table top in your picture and a circle for the birthday cake on it. Do you want to use circles anywhere else in your picture?" Since successful composition depends on repetition and variation, teachers can point out dominant lines, shapes, and colors in the composition and ask which might be repeated or varied, leaving the final decision to the child.

With the more mature children of this age span, it is often beneficial to show them examples of artists' work. A file of reproductions may be kept at hand, and when a child is considering options, such things as variations in texture or alternative means for depicting a sky may be researched in the file.

(Photographs of animals are also handy to have on hand for factual information. They may be put aside as the child continues painting.) Using the works of artists for reference gives children specific, concrete information from the best of sources and helps to initiate the work habit of seeking information from the work of the masters. It also helps to underscore the seriousness of their effort.

Once a child has made a clear commitment to a depiction or means of organization, the teacher should respect it and offer suggestions only if asked for advice. If it is possible to establish the kind of classroom atmosphere that encourages children to weigh carefully what the teacher has to say and then accept or reject it, on the basis of their own judgment, there can be relatively free and easy exchange. But teachers must remember that the burden of responsibility is on them not to overwhelm children with advice and not to hurt their feelings during an activity in which we all, children and adults alike, are very vulnerable.

Responses made at the end of the work period are not intended to cause the child to change a painting but rather are designed to lead to deeper understanding, to reinforce the child's sense of accomplishment, and to prepare for future learning. Thus, they affirm the richness of the narrative and the success of the composition. They can also extend safely into matters of representation, calling the child's attention to a successful figure or depiction of spatial environment. A teacher might point out to Roger, grade 4 (Figure 27), the fine relationship between the sizes of the shapes in the foreground, the middle, and far distance in his painting of "The Airport." It is good to begin building toward the future, by commenting on aspects of imagery a child has used that take the observer's point of view into account, such as the color of the mountain range in "Eskimos Getting Up in the Morning" (Plate VII; Joey, grade 4).

Last, but certainly not least, it is important to recognize the power and nuance of emotion in the child's chosen subject matter. A teacher might say, "Does your dad take you to watch the men picking cotton often? Do you have to go far? Is it hot? Are the fields big? What kinds of machines do the men use? Are there lots of workers? Do they have to work hard? Do you ever help? Do you like to go and watch? Why?" These questions are designed to bridge the child's dawning realization of the very real labor people do to make a living with his personal emotions.

ORDER MAKING AND EVALUATION

Children return to a consideration of the design of the whole surface of the paper during this phase. However, they are not as free as they were earlier to arrange lines, colors, and shapes solely on the basis of design. They are limited by the narrative or idea they have chosen and by the means of representation at their disposal. Narrative is still the dominant of the three strands of painting for them, but they are more and more aware of composition. Their conscious consideration of emotional elements is just beginning to surface. (The latter will be a major issue in the next phase.)

Teachers should expect to see some paintings rich in detail with causal connections between objects, individual objects, and an environment specific to the event depicted. Some paintings should reveal an interest in the relationship of the self to the immediate society and some to societies of other times and places. Some paintings will not include the self at all, as the child is able to relate to more distant objects and events.

Children should be conscious that they are deliberately planning to make a finished and whole painting and should be able to talk about their idea and its composition relatively articulately. They should understand that they are engaged in an act of artifice—that a painting is different from the object it represents and that there are different ways to depict these objects. They should know that they can make deliberate choices according to their own ideas about the subject and about the painting.

In reviewing the progress of an individual, an adult should look for evidence of these capacities and also expect to find in the child's work designs, false starts, examples of efforts to learn the techniques of other children and artists, paintings with simple symbols, and examples of the more complex paintings that they now can compose.

8 Metaphors and Styles: The Den of a Wolf, A Cat on a Cushion

AGES 9, 10, 11

NEW UNDERSTANDINGS ABOUT PAINTING

In his ground-breaking study of the history of representation in fine art E.H. Gombrich (1960) proposed that painters first learn to depict experience by studying the images of other painters. He proposed that artists learn to arrange lines, shapes, and colors into depictions by arranging them into patterns devised by artists who have preceded them. This process Gombrich labeled "making." However, he said that in time artists revise these patterns in accordance with their own changing beliefs and experiences. During some periods in history (most notably during the Realist and Impressionist periods), patterns of depiction have been compared directly against visual sensations and revised. This process Gombrich called "matching." Gombrich thinks of the history of representation as an interplay between the two processes of "making" and "matching."

Children's Making and Matching

As we have seen, children first learn representation by studying images too. However, the images they study happen to be their own nonobjective configurations. Children discover the potential for representation in graphic elements by seeing images in their own designs. Configurations become representations in the mind of the beholder, who thus discovers how to "make" depictions by copying his or her own designs.

The practice of deriving imagery from earlier imagery prevailed in western art until the nineteenth century. (The technique of Renaissance perspective was developed in the studio partially from earlier images and partially from visual observation.) However, in France, beginning with Courbet, Manet, and Degas, Realist and Impressionist painters established the principle of working out-of-doors in front of the subject. They began to rely less on their memory of established techniques for making images and more on immediate perception. They also began to depict specific objects at particular moments in time. These painters discovered that in order to emphasize visual sensation they had to ignore narrative meanings of objects. The meaning of an object in the drama of an event required one kind of imagery, while the visual sensations produced by light bouncing off of it required another. They chose banal, everyday subjects, and the emphasis in painting shifted from the narration of an event to the recording of visual impressions. The fifteenth-century Italian painter, Sassetta, had painted conventionalized mountain patterns for the saints to walk upon; Cezanne, at the end of the nineteenth century, painted Mount Sainte-Victoire for its own sake, from different views and in different lights.

Children begin to create paintings that are representative of a visual scene rather than a narrative, during preadolescence (cf. Figure 32; Leah, grade 6, and Figure 33; Jonah, grade 5). No longer are objects represented by attributes itemized in circles, rectangles, dots, and straight lines. No longer is the picture organized around a story of special objects grouped in special events. Familiar objects or scenes are chosen and depicted by details of their shapes, colors, and textures. In these paintings objects are presented as visual spectacles rather than as characters in the drama of an event. This addition to children's conception of suitable types of images is brought about by their growing recognition of adult art forms and by developmental changes in their cognitive abilities.

Preadolescence

During preadolescence children develop the ability to reason more fully; they are no longer tied to the concrete and can think about hypothetical objects and ideas. Because of this, they are able to combine and organize thought in new, more complex logical arrangements. It is possible for them to stand apart from themselves and to reflect upon their own emotions, actions, and perceptions. They begin to anticipate the future and to deduce probable outcomes. They are able to imagine the point of view of another and to compare it with their own. Their discussions lead to exchanges of points of view, to communication, and to cooperation. Their newfound cognitive ability, together with changes in their physical, sexual, and emotional status, promotes increasing interest in theoretical and social issues. They develop moral codes, debating values on a supraindividual basis and taking great interest in issues of social justice, intellectual truth, and aesthetic ideals (Piaget and Inhelder 1969).

These physical and psychological changes have an impact on children's painting. They can conceptualize the visual appearance of a familiar scene as an appropriate subject for a painting. They begin to include nonconcrete visual phenomena such as shadows and receding planes in their paintings. They begin to represent nonconcrete ideas and emotions by including sym-

Figure 32.   Riverside Drive and 112th Street.   Leah, grade 6.

Figure 33.   My Beagle Hound.   Jonah, grade 5.

bolic objects (e.g., a lonely tree) in their paintings, depicting the pleasures and pains of human existence, as well as moral issues of social justice. The ability to consider things objectively and theoretically and to reason with hypotheses makes a considerable change in their paintings.

Visual Description as an Intention

Children's emerging ability to conceptualize visual description as a goal of painting does not end narrative painting. Children still represent their activities as Michael, grade 6 (Figure 34) did in "Skiing." But even in this painting Michael's increased use of visual detail is apparent. The carefully delineated cast shadow behind the skier resulted from a spirited discussion Michael began during the work period when he wondered aloud, "Do you have a shadow when you are skiing?" The teacher offered no opinion since it was not clear whether the children had begun to understand the theoretical principle behind shadows yet, asking instead, "What does everybody think?" The class debated the issue for some time. Some children took the position that there would be a shadow and others maintained, "You don't have a shadow when you are skiing because you are moving too fast." Michael made his own decision to add the shadow. He also painted pale shades of red, yellow, and blue in bands to suggest the play of colors on snow in the sunlight.

Younger children do not depict light often, and when they do, it appears as a character in the narrative (e.g., as day represented by the sun or night represented by a dark sky). At this later time children begin to include beams of light, but they are still needed in the narrative. For example, a child might paint men robbing a safe in the beam of a flashlight or a dancer caught in a spotlight. Usually this light has a specific beam and a specific source. Preadolescents also make cast shadows, but do not usually paint light falling over a form. (When drawing they are interested in "shading," but their drawings all too often make clear that they do not yet fully understand the laws that govern light.) Ann, grade 6 (Figure 35), painted a simple approximation of shadow on the lower edge of the cat as well as a cast shadow of two values in the "Cat on a Cushion."

Another aspect of visual description is the rendering of details and detailed shapes. An example of children's growing interest in this facet of painting is "My Beagle Hound" (Figure 33; Jonah, grade 5).

The class had discussed the theme of "An Animal You Know Well, or an Animal You Would Like To Be." Jonah described his dog in detail and protested that it would be too difficult to try to paint him accurately from memory. As he began to work the teacher suggested he sketch the dog's shapes on his paper with soft vine charcoal. (Charcoal is easily changed and removed. With it children make shapes large enough to permit being painted. With pencil they usually do not.)

Jonah began with the dog's head and worked hard on the shapes of the

Figure 34.   Skiing.   Michael, grade 6.

Figure 35.   Cat on a Cushion.   Ann, grade 6.

top of the head, the brow, nose, and muzzle. He took particular pains with the ear, commenting on the softness of the dog's ears and how they folded and hung. He continued along the spine, remembering its roundness at the ribs and the curve into the uprightness of a beagle tail. He rendered many details of shape that children of an earlier age would probably have omitted.

Jonah found himself at the edge of the paper as he sketched the tail. He was concerned, but accepted a suggestion to let parts of the dog disappear off the paper. The idea that this would indicate a "closeup" view of the dog made good sense to him. He went on to render the complex shapes of the rump, hock, and legs. All of the legs had to be continued off the paper as he completed the whole silhouette under the neck. This done, he sketched the pattern of markings on the head and back. He began to paint with the same precise care, first painting in the black markings and then mixing just the right shade of reddish brown for the

ear and brow. When these were painted he filled in all the white areas. Finally, he went back to overpaint the mouth and dot in the whiskers.

Now the dog appeared a little lost because its white markings disappeared into the white of the paper. The teacher pointed out that the white paper did not set off the shapes of the dog well and asked, "Can you think of a color that would go well with the others and help the dog to show?" Jonah thought for a moment and said, "Yes—blue." He stroked the blue carefully against the edges of the dog but brushed it freely elsewhere, creating richly colored and textured shapes around the dog.

Jonah's ability and interest in rendering specific details of shape, color, and texture are evident, as well as his ability to make good use of suggestions. It is also clear that he is much more absorbed in creating a visual presentation than in telling a story with his dog as a character.

In another painting (Figure 32; Leah, grade 6) the child is interested in visual presentation of a familiar scene. "Riverside Drive and 112th Street" is a location where her class went to sketch one day. Later, Leah decided to make a painting based on the sketch. In the painting she detailed the textures of the pavement and wall, as well as the light shades of green of the trees bursting into leaf in spring. The painting is landscape for its own sake, rather than a setting for an event. Another example of visual description appears in the careful variations on branches in "Trees in the Country" (Figure 36; Josh, grade 6). The point of the painting has moved even further away from narrative and more toward the delight in the visual sensations created by interesting shapes, colors, and textures.

Images as Metaphors: Ideas and Feelings as Themes

Another pictorial device that appears with the advent of more complex thought is the metaphorical use of images. When children paint metaphorically, they use imagery to suggest an idea or emotion beyond the specific object depicted. Children begin to realize that a picture of an isolated tree suggests loneliness and despair, or that a stag surveying a range of mountains suggests nobility. These sorts of themes are of interest to children, both

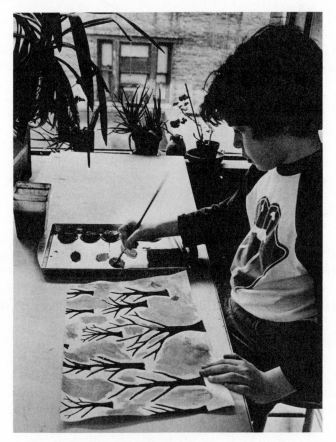

Figure 36. Josh (grade 6) Painting "Trees in the Country."
Photo by Lois Lord.

because they are emotions children are experiencing (or longing to experience) and because children can now consider them intellectually as ideas.

The ability to use visual images for nonconcrete entities like concepts (such as nobility) and emotions (such as loneliness) depends on being able to entertain two levels of symbolization at one time. The artist must decide which object best represents the concept and then which lines, shapes, and colors best represent the object. Children of this period are just beginning to develop an awareness of visual metaphor, discovering the possibility of a second level of meaning as they paint. Whether they are fully aware of the metaphorical meaning as they begin to paint or not, they often produce very expressive images as can be seen in "The Wolf's Den" (Plate VIII; Jill, grade 6).

The painting depicts a mother wolf and her five cubs inside a den. In the center is a soft nest and beneath it a few stony rocks. The den seems to suggest security but at the same time has its rough spots.

The cubs are arranged on the floor of the den in different positions. One is curled into a ball, mouth to tail. Two are lying almost symmetrically opposite each other with their legs twined. The last two are lying separated and alone at the top of the den. Each of the cubs has a long narrow mouth full of sharp teeth and a red glint in the center of its eye. They are much smaller than their mother and yet seem dangerous already. The mother stands at one side, her head raised in a howl. She has the same frightening mouth and teeth. Her eye is deep green with a white glint and her coat has a rough, harsh texture.

The painting depicts a mother caring for her babies, but this dangerous mother howls over her frightening cubs. Nurturance is contrasted with harsh ferocity in a visual metaphor presenting the paradox of the mixture of tenderness and aggressiveness in animals and perhaps human beings.

In another visual metaphor Elizabeth, grade 6 (Plate IX), seems to depict herself in the kitchen with the dining room visible in the distance. The painting is neither a portrait of the cook nor a story about cooking. With its simplified shapes and large areas of soft color, it speaks of the domestic pleasure of cooking and of being a good cook.

It is true that younger children make pictures of fantasy creatures, of battles, of heroes, and heroines and that these refer indirectly to their fears, aggressions, and desires. However, the narrative emphasis and personal quality of the emotions in younger children's paintings suggest that their pictures are expressions of subconscious wishes and fears rather than deliberate visual metaphors.

Style: Limitation of Graphic Elements

The growing capacity for complex thought and particularly the ability to consider aesthetic qualities makes another pictorial phenomenon possible. Children begin spontaneously to limit the graphic elements they use in a given painting to create visual interest and order (cf. Figure 35; Ann, grade 6). In the painting of a "Cat on a Cushion" Ann has simplified the shapes and contrasted a linear textured pattern on the wall with a richer overall texture on the floor. The emphasis on simple shapes and rich textures helps to unify the painting as well as to convey an air of cheerful quietness.

Often stylistic devices are selected to enhance the emotional content of a painting. As we saw in "The Wolf's Den" (Plate VIII; Jill, grade 6), the enclosing circles of the den were painted in soft red and yellow to suggest the warmth and safety of the den. These were contrasted by cold greys and harsh black. Rough textures encircling the soft inner nest were created, in the mother's coat and the rocks. The protective circles of the den were contrasted by the jagged shapes of the wolves. Jill used limitation of color, texture, and shape to help convey the metaphoric message in this very fine example of the complexity of theme and stylistic subtlety some preadolescents can achieve.

Figure 37.   The S.W.A.T. Team.   Charlie, grade 6.

Subconscious Themes

Children continue to make paintings with subconscious themes in spite of their growing awareness of pictorial symbolism. For example, boys often picture thugs or gangsters, as in "The S.W.A.T. Team" (Figure 37; Charlie, grade 6). Here, the members of a Special Weapons and Tactics Team (a sort of police commando squad) rush, machine guns in hand, from a truck drawn up at an intersection to arrest two men waiting under a "Don't Walk" sign. One is very large, carries a briefcase (of money?), and has a cigarette dangling from his lips. The bulletproof vests of the S.W.A.T. team are carefully outlined, as are the details of the cars. The city is dramatically silhouetted against the night sky. In pictures of this type boys seem to be grappling with the question of what constitutes appropriate masculine strength.

Another type of image expressive of emotions first appears at this time. These pictures can only be called "surreal," with their strange juxtapositions of the commonplace and the macabre, bodies as machines, and liberal sprinklings of blood and gore. While full of drama and horror, they also often strike a humorous note as can be seen in "An Eyeball at the Terrace Doors" (Figure 38; Jean, grade 5).

A pair of double doors with a roller blind at their top frames an eyeball. The framing of the doors crosses in front of the eye and disappears into the large black pupil in its center. The eye itself is white with a scattering of nervous red lines to indicate veins. There are some

Figure 38.   An Eyeball at the Terrace Doors.   Jean, grade 5.

accidental drips of white on the door frames because Jean painted them first. The eye has four legs. The two in front are larger, and the two in back are smaller, demonstrating Jean's grasp of the principle that further objects appear smaller. Jean described the dark shape at the left as, "Just a different color." She said, "The eyeball is getting ready to open the door and go out on the terrace." When asked how she had arrived at the idea for this painting, Jean said, "I don't know. We were all just fooling around, and I thought an eyeball on a terrace would be funny."

Though children are usually not clear about the meaning or the emotional motivation of this type of painting, they nevertheless recognize that they belong to a category that the children themselves consider legitimate, if humorous. It may be that the messages in them derive from children's fears and anxieties about adolescence. Many of them suggest the feelings of loneliness or abandonment that growing autonomy often seems to provoke. Others seem to refer to the necessity to accommodate to bodily changes. This eye may symbolize a self wanting to step out and view the world at its feet, yet fearful of being out alone on the terrace at night.

The Representation of Space

During this period children begin to recognize how the position of a viewer influences an image. They begin by being interested in unusual vantage points, such as views from behind a door, through a telescope or binoculars, out a window, or through a key hole. Extremely distant or close-up views, such as we saw in the portrait of the dog (Figure 33; Jonah, grade 5), are also favored. In a painting of a baseball game a very large fielder's mitt and ball occupy the center of the paper (Figure 39; David, grade 5). The ball is so close that we can read *American League, Official Size* printed on it. The ball park is far off in the distance, at the top of the paper.

During this period some children begin to use diagonals to represent the recession of planes in space. However, they usually are not able to understand this device fully and use it inconsistently as Elspeth, grade 6 (Figure 40), did in "Playing My Harp." While the diagonal at the left appears to represent a wall receding, the objects in the space are painted up against the back wall as flat as if they were paper cutouts pasted on it.

Thus, some children begin to understand how point of view influences an image and begin to give up the rectangularity of shapes for the illusion of space offered by a diagonal. However, they are not yet able to relate the two devices to create a consistent illusion. This inconsistency can be seen in Plate IX and Figure 37, both of which use diagonals to indicate receding planes and also depict objects flatly.

We have seen that children's increased capacity for complex thought processes and their physical-emotional development initiates a shift into more adultlike imagery. However, this shift is not fully accomplished during preadolescence. Each of the pictorial devices coming into use is only partially understood by children during this time, and adults must be particularly careful not to assume the child has the ability to comprehend more finished forms. Children are just beginning to adopt visual description for its own sake, as a goal for painting. They are just beginning to use visual metaphors and to limit their use of graphic elements for stylistic and expressive purposes. The devices of point of view and the use of diagonals to indicate recession have just occurred to them. Children must not be rushed to grow faster, but rather helped to do the work of this phase thoroughly and with a sense of accomplishment so that they may progress with a solid foundation.

GETTING STARTED

As children grow older, a teacher's assistance in defining the task and planning an approach to it can become more and more helpful. Furthermore, if a teacher plans the sequence of painting lessons carefully, each task will add to children's knowledge about painting as well as to their capacity to create meaning in imagery.

It is useful for preadolescents to be able to mix a range of lighter and darker shades of any color. They should also be able to make a variety of browns and greys by mixing red, yellow, blue, and white. Neutrals made this way are more subtle than those made with black. This knowledge of color

Figure 39.   Catching a Fly Ball.   David, grade 5.

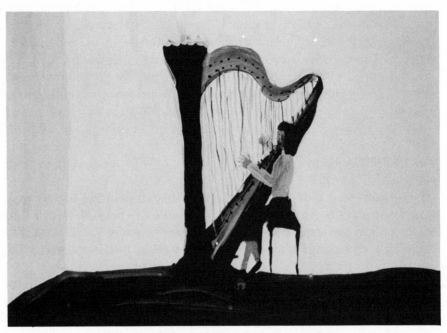

Figure 40.   Playing My Harp.   Elspeth, grade 6.

makes it possible for a child to limit color for style, and to use it articulately for visual description and the expression of mood.

Now lessons can be introduced with questions about subject matter or technical issues. Some subject matter introductions to color follow.

"What kinds of colors do people wear?"
"Where do you go where there are very light colors or dark colors?"
"Which colors in nature are neutral, and which ones are bright?"

If a technical introduction is used the dialogue must be structured to help children formulate a theme for their painting. For example, consider the following.

"How can you make colors lighter?"
"And darker?"
"Are there other ways to make colors darker besides adding black?"
"What is a light (or dark) color that you like?"
"How could you use it in a picture?"
"When you make dark green for the 'get-away car,' you can also make some lighter and darker shades of it to show the shape of the fenders and other details."
"Who has a good idea for a picture using light colors?"
"If you use light green for trees in spring, where will the trees be? What will be in the rest of the picture?"

Since the concept of point of view is beginning to interest children during this phase, themes that suggest a specific frame for a view are helpful, such as a view through a keyhole, a window, binoculars, a telescope, or a crack in the door. Close-ups and extreme distances are interesting and so are striking angles such as an ant's-eye view, a bird's-eye view, a view from backstage, or over a cliff. Many of these themes concretize the position of the viewer and also suggest the drama implicit in sharply articulated points of view. Drama of any kind usually appeals to children of this age.

Discussion of these themes should be limited to what can be seen within the frame but should *not* include any of the formulas for perspective. For example, a teacher might ask David, grade 5 (Figure 39), "In your close-up of the ball hitting the mitt, will the ball park show? Where will you put it?" Exercises in point of view are intended to build up a healthy understanding of this fundamental principle before adding the complexities of perspective to it. Children should not be hurried to achieve a superficial coordination of point of view and diagonals. With a good background of experience now, children will come to use perspective well later on.

It is more effective to approach children of this age span in the format of a general discussion than in an examination of personal feelings. The discussion can begin with generalizations and remain speculative with those individuals who may feel uncomfortable about sharing their deeper emotions. One group of possible themes centers around social relationships and events: the party; alone and together; friendship; and a celebration. Others suggest different emotions, situations or circumstances: something dangerous about to happen; a wonderful place to be; the storm; color for mood; and a new dress, uniform, or outfit. Still others may raise questions about social ideals and concepts: justice; competitions; or discrimination.

The ability to represent people continues to grow and can be helped by painting such themes as angry and kind people; at least three figures in motion; someone being very still; performers (actors, dancers, sports figures); physical strength or a strong personality; people showing their feelings by the way they use their arms and legs.

As with younger children, these dialogues should include some discussion about how specific items of the imagery will be created with lines, shapes, and colors. On the other hand, older children need less help in making the transition from talking to working and in identifying a place to begin.

BEING RESPONSIVE

As in earlier phases, one of the teacher's first tasks is to recognize and validate the interests and efforts of the child. So, during this period, a teacher can look for indications of the additional control of color and of detail in shape as, for example, in Jonah's dog (Figure 33). There is also likely to be a marked increase in the interest and ability of the children to include texture in their paintings (cf. Figure 32; Leah, grade 6). The teacher may comment upon the technique used, for example, "I see you painted a dark color underneath and then painted each of the paving stones later in a lighter color." Or the stylistic limitation of texture for compositional purposes can be mentioned (cf. Figure 35; Ann, grade 6). A teacher might remark, "You scumbled a swirling texture by dragging a dryish brush in little dabs in the bottom, and you scumbled some straight lines in the top. Those textures help to unify the composition."

It is particularly helpful to children to point out the stylistic limitations they have chosen, since they are sometimes not aware of their own decisions. A teacher can describe both the choice of graphic elements and their expressive properties. In discussing a "Cat on a Cushion" with Ann a teacher might say, "You simplified the shapes of the cat and the cushion, made a strong pattern for the wallpaper, and a strong texture for the rug. These make your composition strong and bold, but the shapes and textures you made are soft. The result is a strong painting about a soft and tender subject." This kind of a comment touches on the emotional implications of the subject without forcing Ann to discuss them unless she wants to. It also opens the door for recognition of Ann's use of a visual metaphor. If she replies that she wanted to represent the combined stillness and softness of the cat, the teacher might point out how images can be used as metaphors by discussing the meaning of animals in paintings by adult artists.

Throughout preadolescence, teachers can support children's belief in their own work by showing them how it relates to the work of recognized artists. Their own newly developed ability to think about aesthetic rules and ideals means such questions are very much on their minds. Coming to judge their own work requires a painful transition from personal to more socialized standards. If children come to this transition with confidence in what they have learned, they are more likely to cope well with its stress.

It is equally important that responses to surreal paintings be serious. Even when the painting is humorous or is presented humorously, it has important meaning to the child. Comments should be positive and responsive to the interests of the child without being intrusive. Children will be able to develop ideas of this sort as images more freely if they are not discussed too much. The teacher can validate the activity with interest and by occasional reference to the surrealist painters, showing reproductions and discussing their techniques.

If we reflect on the nature of responses in earlier periods of children's development, what is striking about this phase is the range of possibilities. Children have begun to weave all the strands of the aesthetics of painting together. Visual description has been discovered, and all the fundamental forms of expression have been identified. Teachers are in a position to respond to the wide variety of techniques and ideas that children can now use.

ORDER MAKING AND EVALUATION

At last children are able to achieve aesthetic unity by conscious organization of the narrative, emotional, and compositional qualities of a painting. They have recognized the separate identity of each of these aesthetic strands, can make choices regarding them, and can coordinate the whole. Children can choose to depict a dramatic event, a common event, a distant event, a surreal event, or they can downplay narrative in favor of visual description. They can select and make graphic elements such as warm colors and harsh textures (cf. Plate VIII), softened colors (cf. Plate IX), or simplified shapes (cf. Figure 35) for expressive purposes and can relate them appropriately to a theme. They can choose to paint in an objective style (cf. Figure 33) or in an expressive style (cf. Figure 35). Children have begun to restrict the range of graphic elements to create expressive unity in a composition. They can also select a specific range of colors, lines, shapes, and textures to organize the composition of a painting (cf. Figure 35).

In objective representations children often render many details, making very articulated contours of objects and yet retaining a sense of the inner structure (cf. Figure 33). They have begun to discover that light affects color and creates shadows (cf. Figure 34). The effect of the observer's point of view begins to interest them. In other words, preadolescents are beginning to create representational images using the same visual devices and choices as adults.

Unfortunately, adults (and the children themselves) sometimes compare their work to that of artists and, naturally, find it less accomplished. The very fine work indicative of the culmination of childhood and the less finished work indicative of preadolescence that children make at this time should be evaluated as a step in the development of children's artistic expression. If children are not inappropriately compared to adults, the "decline" sometimes referred to in conjunction with preadolescence will be seen as evidence of growth. These children are beginning to reach for new and more complicated types of imagery as well as bringing the learnings of childhood to their full peak of accomplishment. Their efforts at visual description are just beginning, and as we have seen before, some of the vitality in their work may be temporarily lost during this effort. Teachers should remember the laws of development when evaluating the awkwardness of some preadolescent work.

Children can be helped to value their work during the last years of childhood as a fulfillment of all they have learned. This emphasis makes the transition into adolescence less anxiety-provoking. Children are more likely to remain confident if they have had in-depth training and experience from the start. It is also helpful if they are taught techniques appropriate to their age and given sufficient recognition for their accomplishments. They need the security of knowing a great deal and of being aware that they have a substantial body of knowledge. During this period training in such techniques as representation of figures in motion, neutral and shaded colors, and point of view enhance their security without increasing their insecurity.

Thus, in evaluating children's work, adults should expect some finished and accomplished paintings in which the abilities of childhood are fully realized. There should be paintings with narrative, objective or metaphorical themes, in which the emotional message is clear and the whole is organized into a unified composition. There will also be failed and inconsistent efforts at rendering, particularly figures, faces, space, and three-dimensional form.

Surreal work should be welcomed and respected as a sign of the child's trust in the teacher and courage in trying out unusual themes and expressing internal conflicts. Similarly, narratives with highly dramatic and emotional themes must be respected. They are a sign of the child's growing capacity to conceptualize emotion and should be welcomed despite their often sentimental quality.

In short, the work of preadolescents should reveal the powerful accomplishments in painting consistent with the end of childhood and the first efforts consistent with the transition into adolescence. It is a time for teachers to take satisfaction in the competence and courage of children in using painting for the creation of meaning.

Part V
CONCLUSION

9 Teaching the Creation of Meaning: Developmental Strategies

Children's ideas about painting change dramatically between the ages of two and eleven. What begins as physical manipulation of the sensuous and vivid paints evolves into the depiction of complex stories, the visual description of everyday scenes, and the invention of visual metaphors for ideas and feelings. In the course of this evolution, children use painting to consider deep human problems and acquire the basic understandings upon which artistry depends. As they paint, children are not so much involved in a separate enterprise, "child art," as they are in setting out on the main lines of the inquiry that is art.

Sensitive and thoughtful teaching can help children to develop their capacity to follow through this exciting and meaningful inquiry. Three teaching techniques presented in the earlier developmental sections of this book are especially powerful. These are: 1) dialogues to stimulate children's thinking, 2) responses to their work, and 3) evaluation for the purpose of building curriculum. In this chapter we will review these and other teaching strategies and discuss their usefulness in helping children to create meaning through painting.

ROUTINES AND CLASSROOM STRUCTURE

The purpose of routines is to permit children to be self-sufficient in the classroom and make it possible for them to do their best work. Providing for children's independence involves designing a setup and routine for presenting and maintaining materials that children can manage as smoothly as possible (see Appendix, Painting Setups). Teachers must also make a conscientious commitment to teaching children day after day the routines (see Appendix, Painting Setups) necessary to maintain effective working conditions.

Materials should be of the best, clean, and available. Space should be clearly organized to avoid crowding. Time must be planned to allow children to move through all the necessary processes: getting materials, thinking over ideas, carrying out paintings, and finally, cleaning up. Children also need ample time over the course of the year to learn routines, to explore and gain confidence in their use of the material, and to develop meaningful ideas. The orchestration of time in individual painting lessons and over the year is one of a teacher's responsibilities that requires the most thought and sensitivity.

Children of all these ages need their teacher's time and interest while they work. Teachers of younger children who may have several activities going at one time need to spend time with the children who are painting. Often, classes that do not appear to be interested in painting change strikingly when the teacher begins to give attention to children as they paint.

STARTING THE LESSON

One of the teacher's major responsibilities is to help children become involved in painting so that the activity has personal meaning for each of them. To do this, it is important to consider the phase of development the children have reached. For young children between two and five, it is sufficient to set out the materials in a well-organized and inviting way. However, it will help these young children to focus and to continue their exploration of visual-graphic elements, if the teacher varies the materials and setup from time to time. For example, children can paint on larger paper taped to the wall and on paper placed on the floor. If they paint regularly at an easel, painting at a table will provide them with experience of working in a situation in which the paint does not drip. On some of these occasions they may be offered a choice of smaller papers and on others papers of different proportions. These variations call the size and shape of the painting surface to their attention. Painting with a narrow brush will help children to experiment with the nature of lines, and painting on colored paper will help them to consider color relationships and composition. Each variation on the basic painting activity should be offered several times in succession so that children can explore its implications and possibilities fully.

By six years of age most children need help selecting a personally meaningful "idea" since they do not know what they wish to paint when painting time arrives. Until children are eight a teacher can help the class by asking a series of questions designed to prompt each individual to remember a personal experience of importance. In this discussion, a teacher is not assigning a topic but rather leading the children to focus on an actual experience. This distinction is critical. Questions directed to personal experiences cause children to become involved in meaningful painting, rather than busywork. Consider these examples.

One teacher suggested to a class of seven-year-olds that they paint about "Spring." Predictably the children undertook the assignment with less than enthusiasm; they produced stereotypical paintings of trees and flowers and quickly lost interest. Fortunately, the teacher realized that the children were not involved and began a new approach. The teacher asked each small working group, "What are some of the things you like to do at this time of year?" The excitement of remembering their own experiences involved each individual and they painted subjects as different as roller skating, eating an ice cream cone, and fishing. Each one became involved in an individually meaningful idea and appeared to take deep satisfaction from expressing it. The general suggestion "Spring" was without personal meaning to the children. The focused question asking each child to recall an acutal experience was much more helpful.

Instead of setting a topic by saying "Paint an animal," a second teacher asked, "What animals do you know, or like?" This question helped the children to think about animals they knew or wanted, or were afraid of. Children painted their pet dog or cat, the lion seen in the zoo, and the much wanted pony.

In selecting a beginning question, a teacher considers children's social as well as artistic development. This first question also needs to be concrete enough to interest children and yet general enough so that each child will be helped to think of personal and individual experiences. For children older than eight, questions need no longer be limited to personal experiences but can refer generally to interests of the child. For example, a teacher might ask a group of six-year-olds, "What games do you play?" and a group of eight-year-olds, "What sports are you interested in?" Knowing specific interests of each child will help in formulating questions.

Once most of the children have decided on the experience they wish to represent, the teacher should help children to think about how they will execute their ideas in the material. Each child faces many decisions: What goes into my picture? How shall I arrange the scene on the paper? What size will the objects be in relation to the paper? What colors should I use? These decisions may be made quickly and intuitively or slowly and deliberately, but each one must be considered by the child if the painting is to be meaningful. The teacher can help by asking such questions as: "What shapes will you use (for the dog's head)?" "Will you make your animal (person, truck) big or little?" "Where will you put it on the paper?" By eliciting these choices and decisions the teacher ensures that children think through the process of translating their experiences into the language of paint.

Finally, to help the children make a transition from discussion to action, the teacher asks, "What is the first thing you are going to paint? How will you begin?" The answers of a few children are usually enough to stimulate the thinking of the whole group.

A brief discussion is useful even for those children who come to class excited about an experience they wish to paint. By posing a few well-chosen questions, the teacher will help these children to clarify their thoughts further and to consider the means of translating their feelings and ideas into painted lines, shapes, and colors.

In summary, to invite younger children's full involvement in painting a teacher can set out materials in a convenient and engaging way. In addition older children can be asked a series of motivating questions to help each one focus on a personal experience or interest from which to develop an idea. Once children have identified meaningful experiences, the teacher can ask questions that relate their ideas to the material. Inspired by their own interests and assured that they can translate their ideas into imagery, children will become involved in paintings that have meaning and value.

RESPONDING TO CHILDREN

Once children are at work, there is usually a period of quiet concentration during which each child formulates an approach to his or her idea and begins the process of realizing the imagery. Individual children may have difficulty doing this and need further discussion, but by and large this is a time for the teacher to remain in the background. After children are involved in painting, there are usually a few children who experience difficulty and ask for help. A sympathetic response to the feelings of frustration or uncertainty is helpful, together with clarification of the problem. For example, if an eight-year-old is frustrated by the results of his color-mixing, a teacher might respond, "Did you want to make the yellow darker, and then when you added black it got green too? Yes, that is very irritating, but that is what always happens." This can be followed by assistance in solving the problem without supplying the answer(s), if possible. For example, the teacher could ask, "Can you think of any other dark colors to add to yellow besides black? Try each one and also some combinations of them, to see which you prefer."

It is helpful to offer choices rather than answers. With the younger children only two choices should be offered, as more are confusing. For example, a teacher can ask, "Do you want more little shapes or a big one in your design?" The choices should be matched to the developmental understanding of the child and offered as suggestions for the child's consideration rather than as final truths. This allows the child both to accept those that make sense and to explore further.

The strategy of taking the problem apart (see Chapter 5) is very helpful during these discussions.

Toward the end of the work period or when a child has finished, the teacher can begin to offer descriptive responses. In working with little children for whom an introductory discussion is inappropriate, responses constitute a large portion of the teaching. For both younger and older children it is through these responses that teachers can provide in-depth nourishment of individual children's effort, thought, sensitivity, and technical ability.

In formulating responses the teacher begins by looking very carefully at the work the child has done and by trying to determine the main intention of the child. For example, it might be that a four-year-old seems to have painted a design based on arranging rectangles of different sizes and colors together. The teacher can then describe these with a tone of approval and end with a question to be sure these were important issues to the child. "Look at all the rectangles you made. Which one did you paint first? How did you decide where to put the next one?" Or a ten-year-old may have devoted a great deal of effort to depicting the precise uniform worn by a particular baseball player. The teacher comments, "You put in the color of the uniform, the socks, the style of lettering on the front, even the belt loops. All those details must have been important to you. How did you learn about them?" If the child responds positively, a teacher can share the child's pleasure in knowing the lore of baseball and go on to point out the particular artistic ideas or skills the child has used. It is helpful to remember the child's previous work and to pick out portions of the work in which the child is reaching out for new means of expression. About the baseball player, a teacher could comment, "Look at how you drew the collar going around his neck. It really shows us how strong his neck and shoulders are."

Very young children's sense of design is intuitive. Children from two to five do not have the capacity for speculation or analysis and so cannot describe their plans or intentions well. They are not aware of how they plan a painting even though they may refer to it as a "design." "Design" is simply the word we have taught them to use for nonrepresentational pictures. However, they can, after working, look over what they have done and discuss it with the help of the teacher.

Bringing children's efforts into awareness strengthens and extends their intuitive capacity to think about translating experience into imagery. Through this strategy children become conscious of the choices they have made, their own ideas and skills, and can draw upon them for problem solving in future work.

Responses offered as children are finishing their paintings are optimally timed for learning, because the children's ideas are clear and they are ready to share their accomplishments. Responses succeed best if nonjudgmental and as specific as possible. Any judgment (even "I like it") implies the possibility of a negative assessment and thus can eventually create anxiety. Generalizations such as "What pretty colors" do not offer the child useful information. Some children welcome the opportunity to talk about their work, while others do not enjoy it. The teacher can accept each child's feelings but should try, from time to time, to help those who have difficulty discussing their work to feel more comfortable.

Responses are a very fruitful teaching technique, making possible a number of worthwhile outcomes. They allow the teacher and children to share the meaningfulness of experiences and of the process of making paintings. The conversations that grow from responses help children to establish a sense of themselves as members in a community of painters. They provide children with a vocabulary for talking to peers and adults about painting. They offer children useful ways to think about future work. Most importantly, a teacher's responses recognize and validate each child's experience, feeling, thought, and effort.

EVALUATION

There are several reasons for systematic evaluation of children's work. First, evaluations yield insights helpful in communicating with the children; second, they aid in planning curriculum. Beyond these, systematic record keeping and review supply helpful information to use in communicating with other teachers, administrators, and parents. In the case of painting it is relatively easy to jot down the sequence of lessons and to keep a file of each child's work. (Finding a storage area for the 18" × 24" folders may need a bit of imagination, however.) Most of the children's work can be returned at the end of each review period, with one or two examples being kept for an overall review at the end of the year.

In looking over a child's work, the teacher can establish a good sense of the child's current developmental phase, as well as a picture of the child's progress from phase to phase over time. There should be a range of appropriate themes, with evidence of the child's personal involvement in them. There will be paintings that are well organized and show sensitive use of the material, while some others, reaching into a new phase, are unfinished or less well organized. There should be evidence of growing skill at conceptualizing, manipulating and organizing the visual-graphic elements; and there should be works that convey a sense of pleasure, competence, and accomplishment.

By reviewing the work for evidence of personal involvement, exploration, and a sense of competence a teacher can guide a class successfully from week to week in the creation of meaning.

A FINAL WORD

Children who have not experienced this approach to painting may at first have difficulty with the emphasis it places on their own ideas. However, a teacher's patience in helping such children to adjust to the greater demands that meaningful painting makes on them will be amply rewarded in the end— by the thought, feeling, and vitality in the children's work and working processes.

APPENDIX
BIBLIOGRAPHY
INDEX

Appendix:
Painting Setups

The equipment and materials used for painting should be chosen to offer maximum opportunities for learning, making choices, developing skills, and working independently. A good quality moist tempera or poster paint is superior in color and texture as well as less expensive in the long run than powder paint. It should be used thick (about like yogurt), allowing children to build up textures or to thin it down if they so desire. The colors should be clear and strong.

The primary colors (red, yellow, and blue), black, and white are essential. After the children have discovered how they may be mixed to produce the secondary colors (green, orange, and purple), turquoise and magenta may be added to the palette from time to time, since these colors produce brighter greens and purples when mixed than do the primaries. All other colors may be mixed very successfully from these. Paint in syrup dispensers or plastic squeeze bottles is easiest to pour.

The brushes should be made of stiff bristles (not the soft hairs suitable for watercolors) because tempera is a heavy viscous paint and needs a strong bristle to guide it accurately. Each child needs one flat bristle brush ¾" wide. Another ¼" wide, to be added in time, is also useful. For older children of eight years and up, small bamboo brushes may be used for the addition of details.

Many kinds of paper may be used, but the best standard paper for painting is 18" × 24", 60-pound vellum. This is sturdy white paper that sets off the brilliance and subtlety in the paint. Other papers are manila, newsprint, pages from the newspaper without pictures, grey bogus, brown wrapping paper, and construction paper.

Each child also needs a water container. This may be a can or a plastic container but should hold at least 1 pint to a quart. A cellulose sponge about 4½" × 3" × ¾" is needed for drying the brush. This should not be a nylon sponge, which does not absorb sufficient water.

GENERAL INFORMATION

Color Mixing

Color is a central and unique aspect of painting, and the effort to put children in a position to control color mixing is important. One aspect of this is selecting good paint and another is offering children primaries, black, and white from which to mix other colors. Color relationships based on mixing are invested with a sensitivity and understanding that those based on pre-mixed colors cannot have. Using premixed colors is rather like using a cake mix. The painter has little control over the nuances or the quality.

Washing the Brush

Using one or two brushes and water to wash them encourages the child to select and mix specific colors with care and thought. It allows a child to keep clean colors in the containers and yet to mix at will. Children of three learn to wash their brushes within a few weeks or months if given the opportunity to learn. A few brief instructions (see Chapter 2) and an occasional reminder will be sufficient to offer them this invaluable skill.

If children are painting at easels, a water container and a sponge can be placed at the most convenient end of the paint trough (right end for right-handed and left end for left-handed children, see Figure 10). Small quantities of paint should be put in the paint jars so that they may be easily freshened or changed, enabling children to have clean colors at all times.

The Cookie Pan Palette

Children will gain more skill in color mixing if they have a palette to mix on. This may be a foil pie plate (see Figure 10 in which Melissa, 4:10, is holding a pie plate in her left hand while she paints at an easel). A pie plate may also be placed on a table beside an easel or a rectangular foil container can be pressed into the trough. Children below four often do not take advantage of the palette. All children being introduced to its use should be instructed to "Mix a little pile of color on your tray and then put some of it on your paper; then mix another little pile." This will reduce painting on the tray in the early stages of learning.

An aluminum cookie pan about 11" × 16" × ½" makes an excellent palette. A cookie pan with a lip all the way around is essential to avoid spills. Aluminum should be used because tin rusts rather quickly. The primary colors, black, and white are placed on the tray in furniture casters. (These are the little cups to put under furniture legs available in hardware stores.) Plastic casters 2" in diameter are best. Each caster will hold several tablespoons of color with room left over to avoid spilling. This is usually enough color, and if more is wanted, it may be added either by pouring paint from a dispenser or

CLARK 1981

Figure 41. Counter Setup for Self-Service Painting.

taking another caster of paint (see Figure 41). The sponge, brush, and water container may also be placed on the tray for younger children.

The casters of paint are lined up at the side close to the edge of the paper for younger children while they begin to learn the routines of painting. They are moved to the far side for older children (see Figure 36) who use the tray consistently for mixing. Older children may also move the water off the tray to make as much tray space for color mixing as possible (see Figure 36). Trays and casters should be adjusted to be convenient for left-handed children (see Figure 42).

The cookie pan is very convenient for holding and carrying materials and for making it easy to keep the paints clean and to mix them. It is convenient to use on a table or the floor and may be placed at a table close to an easel as well. It is certainly the preferable palette.

Equipment

The following equipment should be provided for each child.

1 aluminum cookie pan about 11″ × 16″ × ½″ with lips on all sides
5 plastic furniture casters (2″ diameter) to hold paint (It is wise to have several extra sets of casters for extra paints and so dirty ones can be soaked.)

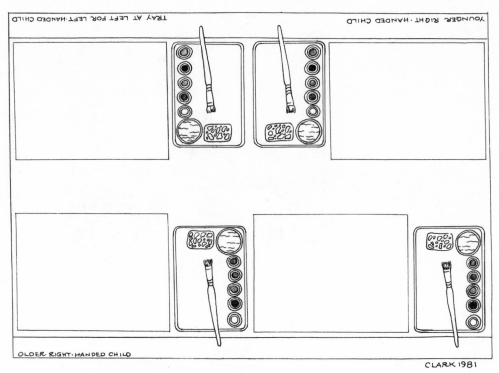

Figure 42. Painting on Floor or Table.

1 cellulose sponge about 4½" × 3" × ¾"
1 flat bristle paint brush ¾" wide
1 flat bristle paint brush ¼" wide

Easel, Table, or Floor?

Working at a table (see Figure 5) reduces dripping paint, helps children learn to build up textures, and to use their hand in painting. There is a tendency for children who work sitting at a table to work for longer periods of time. Working at an easel makes it easy for young children to reach all portions of the paper and to use their arm while painting. Working on the floor (see Figure 42) is good for makeshift setups and large pieces of paper. If a "table" of newspapers is laid down first in a quiet spot, it will help children to avoid stumbling into each other's work. The wall is good for large pieces of paper too. All of these painting methods have their advantages and disadvantages, and teachers will be guided by their own circumstances in choosing those methods suitable for them and their children.

The decision to provide an easel or a table is not as significant as that to provide the necessary equipment for color mixing.

Setting Up

Children of six years and older can help in setting up for painting; younger children can help the teacher set up. Even with older children the routines need to be taught carefully and the children reminded of them frequently. The effort put into this will ultimately be rewarded by the children's increased autonomy.

Routine for Setting Up Tables or Floor

1. One child puts newspapers on tables or the floor. Open newspaper and tell the child to pick up one piece at a time and place it carefully on the tables or floor.
2. One child pours paints into casters (not too full). These are placed, each color in one line, on an extra tray. Additional casters of paint may be piled on top of those of the same color (see Figure 41). Clean casters are kept at hand in a small bucket.
3. One child can put all the necessary materials except the water on each tray and put the trays out on the tables. A separate trip must be made for each can of water even though it is only three-quarters full, until the children are older.

Or

Each of the children can go, one at a time, to the counter and set up a tray. Once again, a second trip is necessary for the water.

Be sure each child has enough room for the whole paper and whole tray to fit neatly on the table (see Figure 42). Tidy and clearly defined working spaces help children to become involved and concentrate on their work.

Discussion

After setting up a teacher should gather children for the discussion. This may take place in a circle on the floor or in chairs in another corner of the room if there is space. Then at the end of the dialogue children can go quietly to their places and begin to work while their ideas are still clearly in mind.

If extra space for the discussion is not available, it may be wise to wait until the end of the discussion to pass out the brushes.

Children should always expect to have some sort of dialogue with the teacher, even if it is but a brief word or two, before they begin to paint.

Cleanup

During the beginning of the cleanup period, each child has tasks to perform. Later, some jobs may be assigned to a few specific children.

CLARK 1981

Figure 43. Counter Setup for Cleanup (No Sink).

Routines for Cleanup

1. Each child shows her or his work to the teacher. If the painting is completed, the child is ready to clean up.
2. Each of the children, one at a time, takes his or her dirty tray to the counter.
3. Each child puts casters with clean color back in their lines on the tray (see Figure 43); older children may stack these one on top of the other to keep them dry overnight. An empty caster is placed at the top of the stack.
4. Each child puts dirty casters in a can to soak;
5. Washes brushes and returns them to the clean brush can;
6. Washes sponge and returns to sponge can;
7. Stacks dirty tray in dirty tray pile;
8. Returns to place to get dirty water and empties can. (The child refills can with clean water and replaces it if another class is expected.)
9. One child washes all the dirty trays. They may be left in a dish drainer to dry.
10. Another child washes the soaking casters after the tray washer is finished. This may also be done during the next class, after the casters have had more time to soak.

No Water in the Classroom

If there is no running water in the room, clean water can be brought into the classroom in a pail labeled "Clean" (see Figure 42). A very small quantity of this is poured into a square dishpan and the bucket is placed out of sight under the table. The water in the dishpan is used until very dirty and then emptied into a second bucket labeled "Dirty" under the table. Another small quantity of clean water is poured into the dishpan. No one should wash or put dirty implements in the clean water bucket. All washing should be done in the dishpan. It often takes children and teachers a while to remember this system, but when they do, the water will go much further.

Makeshift Equipment

For paint containers, jar tops may be used instead of plastic casters. Baby food jar tops are recommended. It is preferable that they all be the same size so they can be stacked. For palettes, aluminum foil pie plates and TV-dinner trays or styrofoam food trays may be substituted for cookie sheets. Each child needs two of these, one to hold the jar tops and another for mixing colors.

Bibliography

Arnheim, R. *Art and Visual Perception*. (The New Version) Berkeley: University of California Press, 1974.

DiLeo, J. *Young Children and Their Drawings*. New York: Brunner/Mazel, 1970.

Dewey, J. *The Child and the Curriculum*. Chicago: University of Chicago Press, originally 1902.

Gombrich, E. H. *Art and Illusion*. New York: Pantheon Books, 1960.

Goodnow, J. *Children Drawing*. Cambridge, Massachusetts: Harvard University Press, 1977.

Kellogg, R. *Analyzing Children's Art*. Palo Alto, California: National Press Books, 1969.

Lowenfeld, V. *Creative and Mental Growth*. New York: Macmillan, 1947.

Piaget, J. *Play, Dreams, and Imitation in Childhood*. New York: W.W. Norton, 1962.

Piaget, J., and Inhelder, B. *The Child's Conception of Space*. London: Routledge & Kegan Paul, 1956.

Piaget, J., and Inhelder, B. *The Psychology of the Child*. New York: Basic Books, 1969.

Smith, N. R. "Developmental Origins of Graphic Representation." Ph.D. dissertation, Harvard University, 1972. (University Microfilms No. 179-9892, 1979).

Smith, N. R. "Drawing Conclusions: Do Children Draw from Observation?" *Art Education*, 1983, *36* (5), 22–25.

Werner, H. *Comparative Psychology of Mental Development*. New York: International Universities Press, 1948.

Werner, H., and Kaplan, B. *Symbol Formation*. New York: John Wiley & Sons, 1963.

Index